Dare to Be Different!

Reflections on Certain Business Practices

James L. Lamprecht
Renato Ricci

D1468720

ASQ Quality Press
Milwaukee, Wisconsin

American Society for Quality, Quality Press, Milwaukee 53203
© 2010 by James L. Lamprecht and Renato Ricci
All rights reserved. Published 2009
Printed in the United States of America
15 14 13 12 11 10 09   5 4 3 2 1

Library of Congress Cataloging-in-Publication Data

Lamprecht, James L., 1947–
    Dare to be different! : reflections on certain business practices / James L. Lamprecht, Renato Ricci.
        p. cm.
    Includes bibliographical references and index.
    ISBN 978-0-87389-777-8 (alk. paper)
    1. Industrial management.   2. Organizational change.   I. Ricci, Renato, 1962–   II. Title.

    HD31.L31518 2009
    658—dc22

                                                    2009035067

Publisher: William A. Tony
Acquisitions Editor: Matt Meinholz
Project Editor: Paul O'Mara
Production Administrator: Randall Benson

ASQ Mission: The American Society for Quality advances individual, organizational, and community excellence worldwide through learning, quality improvement, and knowledge exchange.

Attention Bookstores, Wholesalers, Schools, and Corporations: ASQ Quality Press books, videotapes, audiotapes, and software are available at quantity discounts with bulk purchases for business, educational, or instructional use. For information, please contact ASQ Quality Press at 800-248-1946, or write to ASQ Quality Press, P.O. Box 3005, Milwaukee, WI 53201-3005.

To place orders or to request a free copy of the ASQ Quality Press Publications Catalog, including ASQ membership information, call 800-248-1946. Visit our Web site at www.asq.org or http://www.asq.org/quality-press.

 Printed on acid-free paper

Quality Press
600 N. Plankinton Avenue
Milwaukee, Wisconsin 53203
Call toll free 800-248-1946
Fax 414-272-1734
www.asq.org
http://www.asq.org/quality-press
http://standardsgroup.asq.org
E-mail: authors@asq.org

Contents

1

Introduction

The sobering truth is that our theories, models, and conventional wisdom combined appear no better at predicting an organization's ability to sustain itself than if we were to rely on random chance.

—Richard Tanner Pascale
*Managing on the Edge: How the Smartest
Companies Use Conflict to Stay Ahead*

As we were finishing our book, the financial world was going through an unprecedented economic crisis. In less than three weeks, large international banks in the United States and in several European countries went bankrupt or were kept afloat thanks to major government interventions. As the domino effects of the financial crisis spread to other sectors of the economy, it became evident that a chain reaction was about to impact many businesses. Highly efficient and well-managed businesses were as likely to be negatively impacted by this unprecedented crisis as less efficient or even, as has been reported by the media, grossly inefficient multinational corporations. Our intent is not to study the causes and effects of this global financial crisis on world businesses. Our objective is more modest, and we hope that our comments and observations will help business leaders better withstand future economic recessions. As the economic history of the last couple of hundred years has repeatedly shown, our economic models guarantee that recoveries will follow recessions in an unending perfidious cycle.

The various themes explored in this book came up during a video conversation we had over the Internet. One of us had noted that managers often ask similar questions on how to motivate people, sustain continuous improvement, avoid the overanalysis of too much data, reduce the amount of time spent in meetings, and refrain management from micromanaging.

As management consultants for the past 20 years, we have often heard these and other similar questions. As we were reminiscing over the fact that, as the French would say, "the more it changes the more it remains the same,"[1] one of us sent the following chat message: "It's always the same." To which the other replied, "It's no different than twenty years ago." The outline for our title had emerged.

Yet, although the same fundamental questions continue to baffle managers, we quickly realized that the fact that we were able to have a videoconference from the comfort of our homes (one in California and the other in São Paulo, Brazil) and instantly exchange messages meant that the world of technology and communication had also changed over the past 20–25 years. Besides the Internet, one cannot forget that in the field of management, many promising solutions have been proposed to companies worldwide by experts and popular authors whose ideas have come to pass. The past 25 years alone have seen the worldwide promotion of ISO 9001 certification, the Six Sigma and lean movements (in their various forms), and many other popular movements. Some of these have already been forgotten or are hardly ever mentioned anymore, such as Taguchi methods, just-in-time, reengineering, TRIZ, theory of constraints, and Visual Factory.

In an attempt to better manage their resources and become more efficient, companies also began to spend hundreds of thousands of dollars on sophisticated software programs and

---

1. The expression is attributed to Jean Baptiste Alphonse Karr in the January 1849 issue of *Les Guêpes*.

resource management tools (for example, SAP and MRPII). By the late 1990s or early 2000s, some multinationals (for only they could afford such costly programs) were also convinced to use multilayered, tediously complex planning tools to develop unrealistic strategic plans. The preparation of these plans and the subsequent quarterly monitoring and seemingly unending revisions would in turn absorb many non-value-added resources. When all else failed or did not work as promised, some companies looked into the latest, and supposedly newly improved, human resource methodologies. Coupled with the power of the Internet, the use of keyword filters, search engines, and other sophisticated software analysis programs, these human resource tools are supposed to help companies find the best candidate—one might even say the optimal super candidate—who will efficiently apply the latest management techniques using the appropriate up-to-date jargon to resolve various long-standing crises.

And yet, although over the past seven or eight decades businesses have continuously attempted to reinvent or improve themselves, most are still struggling with the same fundamental questions. In fact, one of our observations is that in many cases, certain advancements in technology, which have in turn influenced management philosophy or their modus operandi, have *not* alleviated a company's ability to answer fundamental questions but instead have often complicated the obvious and have rendered problem-solving activities more difficult and thus more time-consuming to solve.

Although our observations are based on a cumulative 40 years of consulting in quality management as well as work-related experience in various business environments, we are not suggesting that our analysis and observations are all-inclusive, nor are we proposing, as too many authors are inclined to do, that our observations and occasional suggestions are *the best model* that will cure all problems. We know better, and to suggest otherwise would be irresponsible.

THE PREMISE

Our premise is that many companies continue to struggle with the same types of problems (or difficulties) because the same— one could say perennial—factors are present today as they were decades ago. Naturally, with the advent of technology these factors may appear to be different, but our contention is that although technological solutions do help solve technical problems—for example, storing or retrieving data, performing ever-faster calculations, producing nicer-looking tables or slide presentations, and making countless manufacturing improvements—these technologies, including improvements in software tools, do not help people solve problems, become better problem solvers, become more efficient, or reach rational decisions. Instead, they often get in the way of doing the very thing they were designed to do in that they can complicate the obvious. More importantly, these techniques cannot change human nature, nor can they influence office politics. What are some of these perennial factors we are alluding to? They include the following, in no particular order:

1. Employee motivation (a perennial factor identified by researchers as early as the 1920s). Even when threatened by termination, it is difficult to feel motivated in the following situations:

   a. The executive manager, sitting across from you in a meeting, has a base salary at least five to seven times yours and may well have forgotten the everyday realities of the shop floor.

   b. Your manager's incentive and/or bonus package, which will be triggered thanks to your cost savings proposal and initiative, is worth at least 10 times your bonus package.

   c. If cost savings or process improvements are not on schedule, resulting in layoffs, you and others will be the first to be let go; members of management, however, usually get to keep their jobs. And even if some managers are eventually laid off, their severance pay will easily be 5–10 times your severance pay.[2]

d. You know that the solution to a particularly complex problem is outside your control because your teammates have other priorities to solve.

e. If you are a manager or a key player in a process improvement project, you may not be particularly motivated to offer or implement suggestions, because *the metrics used to evaluate your overall performance either may have nothing to do with the project at hand* or may even contradict the objectives of the project.

f. The multilayered managerial corporate structure within which you operate has so many levels and/or is so procedure-bound that the slightest improvement change requires the equivalent of a congressional act for final approval.

2. An unwillingness to take risk that is characterized by rewarding status quo behavior and punishing or at least not rewarding people who try different things but don't always succeed.

3. Increasingly complex software tools that may facilitate analysis but not necessarily provide a solution or resolution.

---

2. A survey of 100 major U.S. corporations conducted by Mercer Human Resource Consulting indicated that median total direct compensation for the CEOs in these corporations was $4,419,300 in 2004. The Mercer study indicated that the CEOs of 100 major American corporations had median bonuses of $1.14 million in 2004, which equaled 141 percent of their annual salaries. In other words, bonuses accounted for more money than the CEOs' annual salaries in this sample. Of course, in view of the recent worldwide financial crisis, these practices will probably change in the near future. http://www.referenceforbusiness.com/management/Em-Exp/Executive-Compensation.html.

4. A belief in the myth of the effectiveness of planning, which in many cases is no more effective than soothsaying. This belief has been reinforced in recent years by the increasing use of sophisticated planning tools that can easily generate immaculate-looking charts and endless metrics. This ability can give management the ephemeral appearance that one is in absolute control of the future, but in fact, these charts are often generated using inaccurate or irrelevant data based on pure speculation. Oddly enough, the paradox of planning, as we shall explain later, is that it is only approximate or effective *when one already knows how to perform a series of tasks.*

5. Training performed when all else seems to fail. Our contention is not that employee training is ineffective (although it often can be), but rather that some training is often conducted as a substitute for problem solving or to supposedly eliminate errors. However, the causes of these errors may be found elsewhere and may even be found in the very process(es) people are being trained on. We must recognize that training, particularly computer-aided training in the form of a PowerPoint presentation, is generally ineffective when it is poorly designed or organized, is too detailed or tedious and hence too long, is delivered too early (for example, weeks before it can be used), or is simply out of touch with the everyday needs of most employees.

6. A new breed of managers who are inclined *to manage from the comfort of their office* using endless spreadsheets and various software and planning tools or who monitor too many useless metrics while at the same time refusing to walk and "see and feel" the process or interview people. These managers are too easily influenced by the high-tech methodology of the month that in most cases is nothing more than a well-established and old methodology that has been recycled for their consumption.

7. Managers and human resource people who do not always know how to find the right candidate for a position and

who, with the implicit knowledge or participation of management, tend to favor people who will maintain the company's status quo. The resulting paradox is that companies end up hiring very experienced people and expect them not to rock the boat or offer innovative solutions for fear of political repercussions.

8. Larger and larger databases that either contain errors or are otherwise inadequate or irrelevant are also a major but all too often unrecognized contributor to a host of decision-making errors. This universal problem can have multiple nefarious consequences for corporations in that (a) it can mislead key decision makers into believing that a problem exists when actually all is well (or vice versa), (b) it can lead problem-solving teams to implement poor or ineffective solutions that are based on erroneous information, (c) it can delay solutions, and worse yet, (d) it can sometimes promote costly erroneous conclusions.

9. Other factors lumped into the general category of "unknown" that we cannot consider either because they are outside our competency or because we are simply unaware of their existence.

WHAT IS OUR MODUS OPERANDI?

The reader will notice that we often precede our observations with words or adjectives such as "in most cases," "usually," and "often." We do so because, unlike others, we cannot claim that we have discovered "laws" of business behavior. We realize that our collective sample of more than 500 companies (accumulated over the past 20–25 years) is but a small sample of all companies.[3] Moreover, we also know that some companies either are better than others or do not commit the same fundamental errors, or

---

3. An example of what we mean by "laws of business" can be found in a remarkable book by Wallace J. Hopp and Mark L. Spearman, *Factory Physics* (New York: McGraw-Hill, 2001 [first published in 1995]).

at least not at the same rate. Consequently, we can speak only of "tendencies" because, as is the case with people, companies have their own unique psychological profile. And although there is a finite number of these profiles, companies will behave and react differently to various situations based on their "character" or company culture.

The format of the book is also different from most other business-practice books in that even though we cite numerous references, we do not rely on the convention of placing notes at the end of the book or the end of a chapter; we prefer the old-fashioned but more reader-friendly and easily accessible bottom-of-the-page format. We have done so for several reasons. First, we realize that the majority of readers who will likely be interested in the topics covered in this book are busy people; consequently, our approach recognizes that less can be more. Second, we've also observed that many books checked out from libraries are only half read; in other words, the last 100–150 or so pages are usually unread, clearly indicating that people ran out of patience or lost interest by the time they reached the halfway point. In view of these observations, we wanted to present our ideas as concisely as possible by avoiding the traditional 250–320-page format of the overwhelming majority of books and thus hopefully increase the odds that readers will read this book from cover to cover.[4]

Our annotated bibliographies not only list books but also offer a summary and include, in many cases, quotations from a variety of authors who over the years have observed or otherwise commented on similar propositions. As is well known, it is often not the best idea that is successful but rather the best-marketed idea that is likely to succeed and be adopted.

Finally, we do not always have suggestions, but for the most part, we limit ourselves to offering observations on what, in our views, does not seem to work or work very well. We hope that in reading our comments, some readers, managers, or even CEOs

---

4. Although the book is around 130 pages, there are only about 90 pages of text; the rest consists of annotated bibliographies.

will be moved to modify their habits and try something else. Of course, we are not offering a cure-all, but rather another way to approach problems that encourages moving away from the status quo, current habits, and method of operation and promotes a desire and curiosity to try something outside the ordinary or predictable. This does not mean that data should not be collected or analyzed, that databases should not be prepared or metrics developed, or that procedures should not be written, employees trained, problems analyzed using software, risks assessed (or rather estimated), processes improved, and so on. Rather, we are suggesting that all of this needs to be done differently by recognizing the *limitation* of each of these techniques, which were never intended to be panaceas for all situations or all businesses. Should one automatically assume that the Toyota Production System, generally known as lean manufacturing, is applicable to all industries? There is little doubt that many of the improvement methods proposed by lean manufacturing are valuable and transferable to other auto manufacturers and, by extension, to many other manufacturing industries. However, does it make sense to apply lean processes in a hospital or a healthcare environment in general? Perhaps in a limited context. But when people's lives are at risk, one should proceed with greater caution when talking about lean processes; in some cases, one may well have to implement redundant processes.[5]

The primary focus of all businesses should be on changing as rapidly and efficiently as possible what obviously does not work or has not worked for a long time. In order to survive, businesses still need to learn to quickly identify the correct problems (with or without teams and preferably without paternalistic corporate guidance), rank them by cost and impact to customers and internal operations, and rapidly suggest and test the validity of solutions for short periods of time before implementing on a large scale.

---

5. One of the authors knows of a nurse who is routinely required to work 60 hours per week and has even had to work a 72-hour week! Are such practices safe for the patient?

2

Always the Same Management Issues

The more we communicate, the less we communicate.

—Richard Farson
Management of the Absurd: Paradoxes in Leadership

The general agreed lesson from the GM experience is that new technology pays off only when coupled with changes in the way work is done.

—Michael E. McGill
American Business and the Quick Fix

Many of the questions, observations, and comments herewith presented have already been addressed over 50 years ago. William H. Whyte Jr. suggested in his influential book *The Organization Man* (1956) that in order for an individual to be more creative in his day-to-day routine, a company should "cut down the amount of time the individual has to spend in conferences and meetings and team play."[6] Unfortunately, Whyte's advice has essentially been ignored. People still spend too much time in meetings or in teams reviewing irrelevant data or trying to solve unsolvable problems and agreeing week after week to meet the following week. When in 1954 Peter F. Drucker

---

6. William H. Whyte Jr., *The Organization Man* (Garden City, NY: Doubleday Anchor Books, 1956), p. 445.

in his classic *The Practice of Management* suggested in the chapter "Decision Making" that "the most common source of mistakes in management decisions is the emphasis on finding the right answer rather than the right question," his advice was either ignored or all too quickly forgotten.[7] Numerous other examples can be found in Whyte's and Drucker's classic and timeless publications.

Although companies are faced with managerial and quality issues similar to those from 50 or even 100 years ago, advances in information or other technologies have had little impact in solving these old problems. Our ability to send e-mails or even have videoconferences with people from all over the world has certainly helped stimulate our ability to communicate instantly, but can we solve problems or innovate any better than our forefathers did hundreds of years ago? We doubt it—in part because in some cases the new generation of managers who were raised in the 1980s playing computer games somehow believe that managing problems is equivalent to playing a video game. All you have to do is click the mouse button as quickly as possible or enter the required data in the latest software tool to know how to proceed to solve a problem or formulate a strategy—just follow the steps precisely and all will be well. As you gain experience and/or master your virtual reality, you'll invariably start winning more and more games or accidentally hit upon the correct virtual solution. Unfortunately, losing computer games does not have any human or financial impact associated with it.

Some years ago someone noticed that the microchip industry was able to double the speed of its chip every so many years. This phenomenon is now referred to as Moore's law. This desire to move or introduce change at an ever-faster rate, driven in part by advances in the Internet and associated industries, seems to have influenced the way business management thinks about change.

---

7. Peter F. Drucker, *The Practice of Management*, 1st Perennial Library ed. (San Francisco: Harper & Row, 1986), p. 351. We also highly recommend the book published by Michael E. McGill, *American Business and the Quick Fix* (New York: Henry Holt and Company, 1986); see the annotated bibliography for an overview.

The need to implement change at an ever-increasing rate of acceleration is perceived as a necessary requirement to achieve success. As many observers reported long ago, this mentality of fast results is driven to some extent by the stock market, quarterly reports, and stockholders who want quick results.[8] Although one must also acknowledge the fact that in many companies changes occur at a crawling pace, it is equally true that in periods of crisis, no doubt induced by too many years of inactivity, managers and/ or executive managers are also often asked to perform like sports coaches, for whom quick results and turnaround are expected within a short 12–18 months. If quarterly performance metrics are not up to par for four or five consecutive quarters, then one must change the staff and eventually the director or manager.

This pressure to show rapid improvements forces managers and directors to impose on their subordinates aggressive and overly ambitious projects driven by irrational metrics or objectives that are unlikely to ever be achieved. These managers set themselves up for failure and then blame others. They go through a round of termination, only to hire someone else whom they think will satisfy their unrealistic plans. The cycle is then repeated. And yet as George Santayana observed long ago, "Progress far from consisting in change depends on retentiveness . . . Those who cannot remember the past are condemned to repeat it."[9]

Could our inability to proceed efficiently when solving problems or crises be somehow related to the fact that many of today's managers spend too much time flipping through solutions much as a teenager pushes buttons on the latest video game? Or do managers spend too much time communicating but not really exchanging valuable information? Could it be that their attempt to direct and/or manage from the comfort of their cubicles or offices is not practical? Or is it perhaps because of the propensity of some

---

8. The financial crisis that began in late 2008 has clearly demonstrated the fallacy of such a model.

9. George Santayana, Chapter 12 of *The Life of Reason*, p. 284. Santayana's book can be read for free at the Project Gutenberg Web site: http://www.gutenberg.org/etext/15000.

executive managers to always want to look at one more Microsoft Excel spreadsheet or one more PowerPoint presentation—acts that require no resolution but consume hours to generate—before reaching an eventual (correct or incorrect) decision? Are businesses now feeling the effect of decades of ill-advised (but well-intentioned), generic, and well-packaged solutions proposed by countless management consultants all over the world? Or is it more a case of companies not using good judgment when trying to blindly implement these arcane suggestions?

THESIS, ANTITHESIS, SYNTHESIS

What is odd, if not in some way amusing, about expert suggestions is that for each suggestion or even for each book, you can find a countersuggestion or counterbook that will either negate or question the original suggestion (Mary Parker Follett made a similar observation 80 years ago). This is not unusual; in fact, philosophers have long written about the thesis-antithesis-synthesis triad, which suggests that for each proposed thesis or proposition there is an antithesis (or antiproposition) that negates the thesis. It is only when the two ideas are combined, resolved, and thus synthesized that a coherent whole is produced. To be more specific, readers will recall that when the ISO 9000 quality movement (some would say a fad) emerged in the late 1980s, it was not long before a few counteropinions began to question the wisdom of forcing every company to become ISO 9001 certified. When Six Sigma (a valuable process improvement methodology that borrows from concepts developed decades ago) became the next fashionable trend, countless success stories began to be published (oddly enough, each telling almost exactly the same account). However, it was not long before a countermovement questioning the virtues of Six Sigma began to emerge. The same can be said about just-in-time (does anyone remember?) or about reengineering (another extremely popular movement of the 1990s that led companies to try to reinvent or reengineer themselves every three to five years).

One of the problems of the past 20–25 years is that companies have been very receptive to one movement or one set of ideas (thesis), only to reject it a few years later (antithesis) and look for yet another set of ideas. To our knowledge, few, if any, companies have ever attempted to synthesize ideas and counterideas whereby they would combine or retain the best elements of what each movement (fashion?) had to offer. We are not suggesting that decision makers—the individuals who decide which trend, fad, movement, or methodology will be adopted throughout a company or a corporation—never acknowledge that something did not work or did not meet expectations. Rather, we are suggesting that instead of analyzing what might have gone wrong and bringing about a *synthesis* of ideas, decision makers all too often decide to call yet another consultant or invest sometimes millions of dollars in a software package (invariably SAP or similar) to help them implement another methodology that they are told is guaranteed to bring results. Unfortunately, although some initial gain may be observed within months of struggling with the new methodology, it is also true that new and often costly problems or modified versions of old problems begin to emerge soon after the implementation is complete. Oddly enough, these "new problems" are often either ignored for months or are not seen as a direct consequence of the new way of doing business—the reflective steps of the synthesis were not performed. The reasons why these decision makers do not attempt to synthesize ideas, simultaneously causing the recurrence of problems, are many:

1. They have no time to reflect, because they are too busy attending too many endless meetings where countless colorful (red, yellow, and green) metrics are condensed in balanced scorecards or dashboard presentations. These metrics are often meaningless because they are too aggregated, poorly defined, or, worse yet, simply wrong. Unfortunately, deep reflection is no longer considered a value-added activity. Quick reaction is of the essence, and it is much more expedient and convenient to click our mouse and move on to another chart, change a color, generate another spreadsheet, and most importantly, start a new problem-solving team.

2. They try to reply to too many e-mails or phone messages and thus rapidly become inefficient while at the same time believing they are achieving much. One of the paradoxes of too much communication is that many e-mails or phone messages are never answered! The increase in communication coupled with the explosion in spam mail has devalued the importance of the message and its content. No time to reflect, except perhaps on weekends.

3. They are required to listen and on occasion, as in the case of high-level executives, feel obligated to constantly interrupt interminable presentations that are admittedly often too long or are so condensed that they provide their audience with little valuable information.[10]

4. They are inefficient because they waste too much time trying to multitask. One of the reasons they multitask is because those defining the job have come to believe that multitasking is a virtue all executive managers and, by extension, all important and supposedly intelligent people are supposed to be able to do. However, the more time you spend multitasking, the less time you can reflect and synthesize.

5. They require problem-solving teams to analyze and solve impossible or overly ambitious problems, and then they are disappointed when the results are delayed or only 50 percent is achieved. And yet, 50 percent synthesis is better than no synthesis.

6. They try to motivate people by using the same team-building model and do not hesitate to exercise their power to nominate or otherwise require people to attend various teams to solve problems—problems that managers have all too often erroneously defined, partly because they have access to faulty databases that warp their

10. For an interesting and informative article on how to prepare a presentation for higher-level executives, see Harold Fethe, "Presenting to the Big Dogs," http://fethe.com/presenting.htm.

sense of priority of importance. Time spent dealing with poorly defined or erroneously defined problems steals away reflective time.

We will now address these and other problems that we believe are partly responsible for the "always the same" symptoms.

OUTSTANDING PERFORMANCE IS INCONSISTENT WITH FEAR OF FAILURE

When, at a party, one of the authors told a retired executive manager that he was working on the subject of why businesses find themselves solving the same problem decades after decades, the retired manager instantly proposed several hypotheses. One of these hypotheses was that only managers who promote the status quo are rewarded, whereas those who are willing to take risks and explore new possibilities are quickly criticized or terminated at the first sign of failure. This observation brings us to the comment attributed to Peter Drucker, that "outstanding performance is inconsistent with fear of failure." This fear of failure, coupled with the expectation that results (whatever their nature but usually based on financial performance) must be achieved within a few months, guarantees that in many cases little will ever be achieved or achieved on time. All that a manager needs to do to keep his or her job is to demonstrate that some gain (imaginary or real) has been achieved; oddly enough, the gain does not have to be sustained for more than one or two quarters. Once a metric achieves the status of green (meaning satisfactory), everyone is happy. However, as is well known to anyone who has charted processes, a metric can become satisfactory (green) or unsatisfactory (red) without anyone doing anything to the process. Such is the wonder of any process—they naturally fluctuate up and down over an average, looking much like a random walk.

In the case of the all-important and carefully watched financial metrics, managers have learned to develop a host of sophisticated techniques to manipulate the metrics to ensure that they satisfy specific objectives (and thus higher management). If that fails, managers have also learned to develop elaborate justifications, usually alluding to some special circumstances, that explain quarter after quarter why a particular metric has gone up or down.[11]

MANAGING FROM THE COMFORT OF THE OFFICE

At the end of World War II (1945) the Ford Motor Company was in a very bad financial situation. The young Henry Ford II was then chairman of Ford and did not really know what to do. Fortunately for him he received a letter from an ambitious and confident young (32 years old) colonel named Charles B. "Tex" Thorton. During the war, Thorton had helped create and staff the Army Air Force Statistical Control Department. This department helped save the armed forces billions of dollars, thanks to the use of statistics and data analysis. In 1946 Thorton wrote a letter to Henry Ford II essentially asking Ford to hire him and nine of his companions from the Statistical Control Department. Ford had little choice and hired all 10 men. Throughout the 1950s and the 1960s, this group of 10 men, who later came to be known as "The Whiz Kids," helped revolutionize management at Ford (and eventually in thousands of companies throughout America) by introducing quantification and decision making based on data collection and analysis, principles they had learned while serving in the armed forces at the Statistical Control Department. This revolutionary style of *rational management*, introduced by the Whiz Kids at Ford, was emulated in the following decades and

---

11. Having observed and listened to many discussions conducted by financial officers, we are amazed to learn how financial performance and, by extension, stock values are arbitrarily derived—this despite the popularity of financial audits that are supposed to prevent such problems from occurring. This pseudorational process consists of having lengthy arguments in the hope of convincing oneself of the reasonableness of unrealistic predictions.

continues to be adopted as the required business model today by companies throughout America and worldwide.[12]

Although one cannot deny that the Whiz Kids brought about numerous positive changes that helped the Ford Motor Company regain market share in the United States and abroad, some serious criticism has been made about the Whiz Kids' quantitative methodology. Some observers have gone as far as concluding that the Whiz Kids eventually became an elitist group ignorant of realities, who managed by the numbers and *only by the numbers*. One of the important mistakes made by the Whiz Kids was that they failed to invest in new equipment. It was not long when, beginning in the mid to late 1970s, Ford and other American automakers found themselves in yet another crisis, namely, the Japanese car phenomenon. Yet to this day, companies continue to follow the model developed decades ago by the Whiz Kids. As companies continue to invest huge amounts of money in the implementation of ever more complex, enterprise resource type software and struggle with tedious planning software tools that generate metrics upon metrics, they have once again failed to bring about a synthesis that would have helped them avoid duplicating the same mistakes made decades ago by the Whiz Kids. The elitism of the Whiz Kids mentioned earlier is still present today in corporate headquarters throughout the world. Young and not so young managers or directors intent on managing companies or divisions with dashboards and metrics are one of the reasons why things take forever to resolve and why things remain the same. More specifically, we believe that the principle of management by walking (not by objectives, as Peter Drucker proposed 50 years ago) has essentially been abandoned in favor of *managing from the comfort of one's office or the conference room*. This in turn has led to a host of associated symptoms that have unnecessarily complicated and simultaneously lengthened the

---

12. In American slang, a "whiz kid" is defined as a young person who is exceptionally intelligent, innovatively clever, and successful.

problem-resolution and decision-making processes in general. Let us explore these issues.

MANAGING FROM THE CONFERENCE ROOM

Increasingly, a new wave of managers (at least in the United States) have adopted the habit of managing from their office. Their decision-making world, facilitated by advances in technology, revolves around the Internet, videoconferences, BlackBerry phones, conference calls, Microsoft Excel spreadsheets, slick Gantt charts or other planning tools, and the ubiquitous quarterly report. All of this makes today's manager a very busy person who is asked (forced?) to multitask as he or she tries in vain to juggle and comprehend situations summarized for him or her by numerous employees who are required to present and summarize mountains of data month after month. The personal and seemingly ancient art of going down in the trenches and asking employees to explain what is wrong with a process or processes is not completely gone, but it has almost achieved the status of an endangered species. Some executive managers still try to schedule sessions once or twice a year with nonmanagement personnel to get a feel for what might be wrong, but these four-to-six-hour sessions are but an infinitesimal portion of the time spent on all other activities. One would hope that the task of interviewing people to find out what is wrong with a process would be taken up by members of the problem-solving team, but even here the tendency is to first analyze and reanalyze data ad infinitum using increasingly sophisticated statistical software tools; the comfort of nonconfrontational databases is so much more appealing. We will return to the problem with databases, but first let us explore the limitations of multitasking, or the art of doing many things poorly.

THE PROBLEM WITH MULTITASKING

The glorification of multitasking, perceived as an essential talent and a required skill of all efficient managers or white-collar workers, is a relatively new phenomenon that became popular about

15 years ago. Prior to its application to human activities, the word "multitasking" had been used as early as the 1960s. It was used in the field of computers, where it referred to the computer's ability to perform simultaneous tasks or what appeared to be simultaneous tasks. Actually, in the early days of computer timesharing, when computers were "asked" to multitask, one could clearly see the effect of multitasking on the central processing unit. As more and more users signed on to use the computer, the response time increased. As you sat in front of your terminal, you would notice that when you pressed the "Return" key, the computer would take longer and longer to acknowledge your command. Eventually the computer would crash and the system would have to be restarted because of too many users—too much multitasking. The efficiency of the computer *decreased* with multitasking. The same applies to humans.

As companies began reengineering their processes in the early 1990s, they simultaneously began eliminating job titles and combining jobs, thereby producing interesting titles such as Quality, Health & Safety and Environmental Manager or Financial and Accountability Supervisor. With the scope of responsibilities expanded, multitasking was seen as an essential requirement in job performance. It is so common today that it is often listed as an essential skill. But is the supposed ability to multitask indeed a virtue as we are so often led to believe? Moreover, can we truly efficiently multitask?[13]

It is true that some professions require the ability to multitask. For example, a piano player can read and play music written for two different keys using the right and left hands. An organ player needs to simultaneously read three parts (left and right hands and feet). A drummer can also keep two or three different beats (simultaneously). But few other professions can perform

---

13. We do acknowledge that many people are quite capable of writing an e-mail or performing some similar task while at the same time half listening (or not even listening) on a conference call; still, while typing their e-mails they are not concentrating on what is being said in the conference.

more than two or three tasks at the same time without making mistakes or slowing down considerably. Some professional jugglers can juggle seven balls at the same time, but even then they can do it only for a few seconds. However, these are the exceptions rather than the rule.

The fact is that when we think we are multitasking, we are actually performing one task at a time and are constantly switching back and forth between the various tasks, thus slowing down our thinking. An increasing amount of time is spent "swapping" back and forth (early computers did the same thing and gave the appearance of simultaneous multitasking only when the cycle time between swaps was reduced). Moreover, people who think they can perform efficiently while supposedly multitasking are in fact performing at a slower rate of efficiency and are more prone to commit errors. For those of you who still think you can multitask efficiently, let us remind you that people who talk on their cell phone while driving will invariably (and thankfully) find themselves slowing down. Their brains are too busy trying to multiprocess, which forces them to do the next wisest thing to hanging up, they slow down. Many accidents are due to people being on their cell phone while driving.[14]

Of course, when people refer to the ability to multitask, they generally mean the ability to work on more than one project at a time, an ability that has no doubt existed since the dawn of time. Nevertheless, beyond three or four projects, people start to rapidly lose efficiency as they find out that more time is now required to review each project. A consequence of such multitasking is that each project now takes longer to complete because what was gained by a synergy of focus is now lost to time spent swapping between projects.[15]

---

14. http://www.newsdial.com/technology/communication/cell-phone-statistics.html

15. If you do not believe this argument, you may want to check the following Web sites or do your own Internet search for the words "multitasking and efficiency." Among the many references you should find are http://www.apa.org/releases/multitasking.html and http://www.apa.org/monitor/oct01/multitask.html.

THE LIMITS OF VERBAL INTELLIGENCE

The limits of verbal intelligence refers to the practice of using words or acronyms in conversation or in meetings without really understanding their meaning and thus giving the impression that we know what we are talking about. We are all guilty of having used certain words without being able to define them. However, within a work environment, verbal intelligence can cause undue stress and cost tens of thousands of dollars, if not more, whenever it is used.

Many managers and non-managers have developed verbal intelligence in many domains over the years. In order to survive in a world where trends and their associated jargon may have a half-life of only two to three years, they have had to acquire an extensive vocabulary of words that are perceived as being essential to good and effective management. In quality management, a sample of these words (not intended to be inclusive) includes Six Sigma, DMAIC (define, measure, analyze, implement, and control, the basic methodology of Six Sigma), kaizen, kanban, lean or Lean-Six Sigma, and Toyota Production System (TPS), which is not to be confused with the dozens of other meanings associated with the similar acronym TSP. Let us not forget ABC costing, cost-benefit analysis, and risk analysis or risk management, as well as a host of acronyms that are believed to differentiate between knowledgeable managers who can perform and lead people and vocabulary-poor underperformers.[16] The problem with this logic is that using a word in the right context does not mean that one understands the subject matter. Worse yet, when the words or acronyms refer to a methodology (rarely new and all too often

---

16. The problem with acronyms is that they can mean many things. For example, TSP could stand for, among other things, "traveling salesman problem," "telecommunication service priority," or "team software process," whereas TPS generally stands for Toyota Production System, associated with lean manufacturing. However, for a software engineer, TPS means "test procedure specification." Many other definitions are listed at http://acronyms.thefreedictionary.com/TPS.

recycled), little or no knowledge of what the word or acronym means invariably leads to devastating and costly outcomes that are guaranteed to frustrate many individuals. Superficial knowledge, misunderstanding, or misapplication, caused in part by a dangerous use of verbal intelligence, is one of the major causes of frustration in industry. Verbal intelligence does not help solve problems that are, or should be, major concerns of managers; it only obfuscates the problem, which is further exacerbated by easy access to Wikipedia or the Internet in general.

There is yet another important issue relating to verbal intelligence that needs to be explored: the use of keywords to define job skills. Ever since the development of specialized job sites on the Internet that allow people to search for jobs in any city, the nefarious effects of verbal intelligence have been amplified. In order to supposedly better filter job applicants, it is now common practice by headhunters, human resource specialists, and others to use a series of keywords to not only define a job requirement but also help candidates search for particular jobs. The unfortunate side effect of this practice is that numerous keywords are automatically appended to a job description whether or not the skills are needed for the job; in other words, when in doubt, ask for everything. The resulting habit of trying to encapsulate a set of skills by using a set of keywords such as "lean manufacturing experience" or "Minitab experience," or worse yet, listing as many as 30 or more synonymous keywords, is reductionism par excellence.

The erroneous presumption made by potential employers is that unless a candidate can recite a list of keywords sprinkled with a few case studies from Web sites, the candidate is automatically assumed to be not qualified, or at least not ideally suited for the position. This irrational assumption, which reduces skills or abilities to a set of keywords, also reduces the opportunity to hire candidates who may have similar or even more experience but who cannot recite the appropriate and approved list of words; in other words, the required skills to do a job are now linked to one's ability to speak the jargon. Of course, this is not yet a sufficient condition, but it is a necessary prerequisite. Thus whenever one applies for a job that lists as one of the requirements "lean manufacturing experience," the candidate should be able to talk about and give examples of, among other things, value stream mapping, 5S or 6S, 3P, kanban, and poka-yoke. To further impress the interviewer, and at the risk of compromising his or her credibility, the candidate could also talk about his or her experience with the Supply Chain Responsiveness Matrix (or better yet, use the acronym, SCRM) or talk about his or her work with "demand amplification in the supply chain" and perhaps even casually mention the name Jay Forrester. The more acronyms one can mention, the more one differentiates himself or herself from other candidates and thus potentially impresses the interviewer. Of course, we are not suggesting that name dropping is sufficient to be hired—one would have to be able to back up the name dropping with some case studies. But thanks to the vast resources of the Internet, that is no longer too difficult to do.

How is the practice of reducing jobs skills to keywords related to the "it's always the same" syndrome? We will answer that question in a subsequent chapter.

OTHER RELATED ISSUES: MANAGING AND MAKING DECISIONS WITH POWERPOINT

Much has been written about the inefficacy and limitations of PowerPoint presentations (see, for example, the many contributions of Edward Tufte). We will not repeat those arguments here, but instead observe the following:

1. Computerized presentations are naturally time consuming to prepare and to watch, not so much because much information is necessarily included (although this can be the case) but because too many people think that pretty, colorful graphs must be included, especially in presentations made to high-level managers. Graphs can be helpful, of course, but tables can be more concise and can better show relationships that would require either several graphs or, worse yet, three-dimensional graphs

that are difficult to interpret when sitting in the back of a conference room.

2. Computerized presentations reinforce the tendency of certain managers to manage from the comfort of the conference room, in addition to managing from the comfort of the office. Eight to twelve people can converge in an air-conditioned room furnished with comfortable chairs and beverages and can be entertained or bored to death (depending on the presenter) with slides upon slides of facts, graphs, figures, and milestones. And let us not forget the now ubiquitous tri-color (red, yellow, green) metrics that (supposedly) help all present quickly assess or even master the gravity of any situation, much as a traffic light can control traffic.

3. Behind every metric is a lot of information, reasons, or events that *may* explain why the metric is what it is (good or bad). Unfortunately, all of this background or contextual information is lost, buried, or engulfed by the mystical power of a metric that averages, summarizes, flattens, and thus ideally represents the status of a complex process in green (satisfactory), yellow (warning), or red (danger or unsatisfactory) colors. Of course, this does not mean that during a presentation, clarifications are not provided as to why a particular metric went up or down. In fact, a presenter must often spend a considerable amount of time to justify, clarify, or simply explain why in the past two to three months a particular metric went up or down.

THE PROBLEM WITH TOO MANY METRICS

The use of the balanced scorecard, proposed in 1992 by Robert Kaplan and David Norton, is a good example of a reasonable idea that has gone terribly wrong. To produce balanced scorecards, companies all over the world began to attach metrics to every process (the early history of such attempts at Ford by the Whiz

Kids was discussed earlier in the chapter). This practice of generating excessive information has led to some unfortunate and unforeseen consequences.

One cannot deny that metrics, when carefully chosen and clearly defined, are valuable. For it is true, as has been observed countless times by innumerable consultants and management gurus, that if you cannot measure a process, you cannot assess or change its status. And yet, would metrics have explained or uncovered the financial debacle that occurred in September 2008? Perhaps. But then again, this assumes that the metrics are available for public review and that the public would have understood their meaning. It should be pointed out that a few financial experts did know how to interpret these financial metrics, and they began to express serious concerns as to the health of the financial market as early as the first quarter of 2008 or even late 2007; sadly, their minority opinion was ignored.

Regarding excessive quantification and/or "metrication," Ford executive management discovered more than 35 years ago that:

1. We should be aware of our limits to quantify certain key drivers, such as product quality, customer loyalty, innovation, or competitive advantage, to name but a few.

2. Even when we can accurately quantify key drivers, we are then required to include in our calculations forecasts of their effects well into the future.[17]

Unfortunately, when consulting firms and consultants in general preach to companies the virtues of quantification and developing metrics for just about everything under the sun, they teach only half the story. Indeed, as Herbert Simon observed long ago, "What information consumes is rather obvious: it consumes the attention of its recipients. Hence a wealth of information creates a poverty of attention, and a need to allocate that attention effi-

---

17. http://www.amnesta.net/other/whizKids.

ciently among the overabundance of information sources that might consume it."[18]

The problems with metrics are many and begin when:

1. You have too many metrics. Companies that have developed performance metrics or other types of process metrics have quickly found out that they now have metrics for everything. In fact, they have so many metrics that they cannot manage them all. This is certainly not a new problem. In the 1950s, corporations such as GM had rooms full of statistical process control charts. If anything, the increasing use of computers has exacerbated the problem. Managers have an increasingly difficult time "seeing" the relationship between metrics and/or they cannot digest the meaning or significance of all these metrics. Consequently, they tend to ignore most metrics or rapidly review them and focus on a handful of red metrics. This is a natural consequence of wanting to measure everything. Moreover, when we recognize that presenters usually have no more than 10–15 minutes for their presentation to executive management, the task of reviewing more than five or six metrics per department becomes impossible. A corollary is that since managers are increasingly busy, they do not have time to look at all these metrics. Yet, they often ask for more information in the form of more data. Thus it is not uncommon to see that even if a presenter includes a vast array of tables in the presentation, managers will often ask for yet another set of tables to answer one more question. Asking more questions (relevant or irrelevant) is easy; solving problems is more difficult.

---

18. Herbert Simon, in *Computers, Communications, and the Public Interest,* ed. Martin Greenberger, pp. 40–41 (Baltimore: The Johns Hopkins Press, 1971).

2. Important decisions are made on poorly defined metrics (that is, metrics that are too aggregated and therefore too vague) or when inaccurate (error in calculation) or wrong metrics (error in formula) are generated. Suffice it to say for now that many problem-solving teams have been ordered on costly ventures by management to try to analyze why a particular metric reached a supposedly unacceptable level, only to find out that the problem was not so much with the process but with the metric "describing" the process.

3. Industry-wide metrics are used for the purpose of comparing (benchmarking) performance. Company executives and management often make the erroneous assumption that the metric (for example, warranty cost, on-time delivery, percent accurate inventory count) has the same definition across industries or even within the same industry; unfortunately, this is not the case. When one of the authors worked on a warranty cost reduction project, it became evident that one could not compare warranty costs across industries, nor could one compare warranty costs within an industry, because each company has its own warranty accounting practices that directly impact how warranty costs are computed and eventually reported.[19] Consequently, executive managers or directors should exercise great caution when they arbitrarily state, "We should lower our warranty cost to match the XYZ company." Before expressing such demands, it would be prudent to first try to determine if both companies have the same warranty accounting practices. But since this information is unlikely to be

19. An excellent series of articles is available on the Warranty Week Web site at http://www.warrantyweek.com/archive/ww20050308.html. See "Warranty Conference, Part One," where the issue of warranty accounting practices is discussed.

shared by any company, it would be wiser to first calculate warranty costs for a period of three to five years and, assuming no new products were introduced during that period of time, proceed to establishing a reasonable warranty cost target (see "The Case of the $3.7 Million Warranty Cost Reduction" in Chapter 6).

4. Metrics are reviewed too frequently. Yet another related problem is the frequency with which metrics are reviewed. In some companies, metrics are reviewed weekly! In one multinational company that one of the authors worked with, management wanted to react whenever a trend was detected. Reacting to trends is certainly commendable; however, when a trend is defined as two consecutive points, such an overreaction defeats the purpose of monitoring any process. As has been known for well over 60 years, constantly adjusting a process (or reacting to a process) increases rather than decreases its variation. The magnitude of this "overreacting crisis" in many companies is magnified exponentially with the number of metrics. Indeed, one can suggest the following:

Too many metrics → too much monitoring → too much reacting whenever one or more metrics go outside their arbitrarily defined limits. This in turn leads management to create problem-solving teams to investigate what went wrong. But in fact, nothing may have gone wrong, as the unacceptable fluctuation in a metric may be caused by a mere random fluctuation. If nothing is wrong and the process is actually in control and stable, the spikes will soon decline and stabilize once again around the average.

The managerial habit of constantly wanting to react to (too many) metrics is in direct contradiction to the principles of lean manufacturing. Indeed, what executive managers and their direct reports must come to understand is that there is a pressing need in corporations throughout the world to adopt what could be referred to as *lean managerial practices*.

LEAN MANAGEMENT: A NEW APPROACH FOR BUSINESS LEADERS

The following events describe real practices witnessed by one of the authors while working for a company. The practices of managerial control described herewith are certainly not unique to this company, but they could be perceived as extreme. To maintain anonymity we shall refer to the organization as Company Y.

The Case of the Weekly Meeting

Company Y is very database oriented, which is not unusual for many companies nowadays. In this particular instance, however, the level of monitoring and control exercised over managers is surprising. By way of introduction, we should explain that the quality management system of Company Y consists of hundreds of corporate procedures spread over three or four databases and includes a vast array of additional procedures that are wrongly perceived as necessary ISO 9001 requirements. In addition, there are hundreds of additional local procedures. These local procedures are, in many cases, slightly modified versions of the corporate procedures that have been adapted to the needs of each customer. In some cases, the procedures are nothing more than a reference to a spreadsheet. We should also point out that Company Y firmly believes (perhaps paradoxically) in applying the principles of lean manufacturing and has appointed a senior director of operational excellence, who is not shy about using a plethora of planning charts to monitor the simplest lean event. Now that you've got some background on Company Y, let's return to the "case of the weekly meeting."

Every week each manager is required to enter on an electronic worksheet the number of hours he or she worked on a project. This is not unusual, except that almost the identical data have to be entered into a second database. In the second database, each manager must reenter how many hours he or she worked (the information is already logged in a timecard database) and must also estimate how many hours he or she will work the following week. In addition, each manager must answer questions on a

Microsoft Excel spreadsheet (colored with the required red, yellow, and green options) that ask whether additional resources are needed, whether the project is on time, whether help is required, whether the individual has some free time to help others (this is very unlikely, and it would be professional suicide to even admit to such a thing), whether the individual has any vacation or traveling planned, and so on. This must be done every week. Having performed this data entry usually on a Friday afternoon, the manager must then join a conference call every Monday morning. This conference call can occasionally last up to 90 minutes, but it usually lasts 60 minutes and is attended by no less than 27–30 managers. What is rather amazing is how the meeting is conducted.

The director who calls these Monday meetings usually spends 10–12 minutes talking about various so-called dashboard events. This means that in the best scenario, 45–50 minutes is left for the other 25 or so attendees. Each participant spends, on average, no more than a minute and a half talking during the meeting. But that is not all. What is even more remarkable is that each participant spends about one minute reading the information that was entered on the spreadsheet the previous Friday! So, every Monday, everyone has to listen to upward of 25 people saying that they worked 42 hours last week, that they plan to work maybe 44 hours this week, that they do not need help, and so on—information already available to the director on his spreadsheet. And then, amazingly enough, each manager must state what his or her greatest achievement was for the previous week—"I conducted an internal audit," "I met with so and so," "I finished this or that project," "I am on target with my project"—and provide other such apparently invaluable details to the director. These achievements are also listed on the spreadsheet, but oddly enough everyone must read them for the "benefit" of the others. Week after week a group of managers quietly submit themselves to this odd ritual of inefficiency, and a few (including, obviously, the director) even think this is an invaluable activity.

Not only do we find the need to read what is already entered in the spreadsheet of dubious value, but the expectation to recite weekly achievements to a group of managers is equally incomprehensible and of no value except perhaps to the director, who already has all the information available to him. Defenders of this managerial ritual could suggest, but hardly convince, that this level of detailed information is relevant or perhaps important to the director. But the problem with this suggestion is that in his attempt to be productive or be perceived as being productive (or as is colloquially referred to as being "on top of everything"), the director actually inconveniences and reduces the efficiency of as many as 27 people for up to an hour every week.

The Cost of Meetings

Let us estimate the cost of these Monday recitations based on the following assumptions or facts:

1. Meeting duration: one hour
2. Preparation for meeting (entering data, logging in): 15 minutes, for a total meeting time of 1.25 hours per week
3. Assume a rate for manager of $65/hour
4. Assume that, on average, 27 managers attend each week

We have the following: 27 managers × 1.25 hours/week × 52 weeks × $65/hour = $114,075 for 1755 hours of meetings just to hear people recite, among other things, their weekly achievements—not exactly a lean event! In case the reader might have forgotten, these estimates are only for Monday meetings. If these costs do not seem absurd, then nothing is absurd.

The level of control does not end here, because there are also various dashboards to review with the inescapable red, yellow, and green statuses. One could also talk about the manager who called a three-hour meeting to review the 198 steps listed in a planning spreadsheet. The number 198 is not a typographical error; the plan had 198 steps, and just about every step was 3, 5, or 10 days. The manager in question was apparently not aware of the concept of critical path, nor did the manager realize that it would be impossible for one, two, or even three people to finish all those tasks in the required (and unrealistic) 45 days. However, everyone attending the conference call went along and played the game. Such are the unfortunate consequences of using "easy to use" software applications without knowing the theory or methodology behind them; simply click on the application and you are on your way to generating tables upon tables or charts upon charts of output to be reviewed by managers upon managers week after week.

The habit of not questioning irrational behavior or simply "going along with the program" is certainly not uncommon; in the best economic times people generally do not want to offer critical comments. When faced with a monolithic corporate bureaucracy, people tend to naturally feel overwhelmed and freeze into complacency or inaction. People will often tell you that what they see around them is "absurd," but for political reasons or simply job security no one dares offer any suggestions or question current practices during a meeting. It is, of course, safer to go along and rely on the wonders of the pharmaceutical industry to try to control one's blood pressure. Consequently, everyone must endure these irrational rituals week after week.

The concept of lean management that we wish to propose assumes as its major premise that, before creating a new activity, management should reflect on the following three questions:

1. What is the objective of the activity and how much is gained by its execution?
2. What are the costs and benefits of executing the activity?
3. How can one execute the proposed activity in the simplest, most cost effective and objective way?

Lean management should focus on activities that generate real value and innovation. As we saw in the earlier example, some (many?) meetings are simply a waste of precious time. We will explore this theme further in the next chapter.

CONCLUSION

Some authors over the years have tried to explain why the use of various management tools supposedly designed to help companies "transform" themselves has produced very little results. One such author, Richard T. Pascale, explains that "the trouble with 'transformation' is that it has been relegated to the questionable status of muddled, New Age thinking. In part, this is because we keep trying to apply the *tools* of the transformation without a corresponding shift in our managerial *mindset*." Obviously, such an approach cannot work, because, as Pascale concludes, the law of requisite variety states that "for any system to adapt to its external environment, its internal controls must incorporate variety. If one reduces variety inside, a system is unable to cope with variety outside." Too many high-level managers continue to ignore this problem and persist in repeating the same errors that will never be solved by periodically throwing slogans at problems.[20]

Annotated Bibliography

Adams, Scott. *Dilbert and the Way of the Weasel*. New York: HarperBusiness, 2002.

Adams is the creator of the famous cartoon *Dilbert*. Much of what Adams has to say is taken from the thousands of e-mails he has received over the years from people working in corporate America. His comments are often very witty and rarely wrong. Here are a couple of examples regarding consultants and Six Sigma:

> First, because consultants are involved and consultants charge by the hour, you can be sure that the number of meetings increases exponentially. Consultants have to sell their service to get in the door. That means they must convince senior management that Six Sigma is "new" and that companies that used it do better than those that don't. (213)

---

20. Richard Tanner Pascale, *Managing on the Edge: How the Smartest Companies Use Conflict to Stay Ahead* (New York: Simon and Schuster, 1990), pp. 13, 14. The law of "requisite variety" is explained in W. Ross Ashby, *An Introduction to Cybernetics* (London: Chapman & Hall, 1956).

When I heard that GE and Motorola were using Six Sigma, I knew it must be the sort of virus that prefers a large bureaucratic host—the kind of place where it's unwise (to be) the one to identify a "problem" with the current way of doing things. Once you have your Six Sigma program in place, you can take credit for any lucky thing that happens in the industry while blaming the industry itself for any unlucky things. (212–213)

Here are some other pearls of wisdom on planning, objectives, and statistics:

When you lie about the future, that's called optimism, and it is considered a virtue. . . . When you apply this unique brand of optimism (not lying!) at work, that's called forecasting. (83)

You want objectives that could be accomplished by a squirrel in a coma. (21)

"Statisticians rarely write management books because they know that a certain number of morons will succeed under any system by pure chance" (167). Adams refers to these managers who are at the right place at the right time as "world-class managers." It is difficult to disagree with such insight.

McGill, Michael E. *American Business and the Quick Fix*. New York: Henry Holt and Company, 1986.

This excellent little-known nine-chapter book reviews many of the management myths from the 1940s–1980s. A brief chapter-by-chapter overview of some of McGill's major ideas is listed below.

1. Introduction: Myth and the Modern Manager

Some of the then-famous fads and fixes listed by McGill over a 40-year period include zero-based budgeting, Slinky, T-group sensitivity, pet rocks, hot pants, centralization, management by objectives (MBO), and corporate culture. McGill asks the reader to guess when the fad or fix was introduced. He comments that young people often think that their fads are different and that they will last (3). Corporate managers don't like to see their fads compared to pet rocks.

2. Forty Years of Fads and Fixes

In this chapter McGill reviews the few fads and fixes introduced over the years. MBO was introduced by Peter Drucker in 1954. PERT charts (now popularized in various software) were introduced by the U.S. Navy in 1957–1958 for the Polaris submarine project and adopted by firms like Ford, but as McGill observes, management could not handle the "sheer weight of the paperwork required by the systems" (11). As for MBO it was "a simple, popular solution that, once put to the test, did not meet managers' needs *and*, to make matters worse, took a tremendous amount of paperwork to accomplish" (12). (Note: Naturally, admirers of Peter Drucker would disagree with McGill's assessment; see, for example, the book by William A. Cohen, *A Class with Drucker: The Lost Lessons of the World's Greatest Management Teacher* [New York: Amacom, 2008]. The book offers a good overview of Drucker's philosophy and ideas.)

T-Groups, or sensitivity training, were popular in the 1960s and 1980s (a sort of psychotherapy used on managers). Managers were supposed to be concerned for their people and for production. McGill makes an amusing reference to the blind squirrel phenomenon, which suggests that once in a while even a blind squirrel will find a nut.

With zero-based budgeting (popularized by Robert McNamara at Ford), the use and/or meticulous completion of forms became the all-important activity. The Boston Consulting Group introduced strategic planning in 1970. McKinsey & Company introduced the Seven S's: strategy, structure, system, staff, style, skills, and super-ordinate goals. These terms were supposed to describe the success of the Japanese firms. The Seven S's should not be confused with the popular 6S methodology, which first appeared in the late 1980s and early 1990s (23).

Using videotapes (today DVDs and Web videos) to market fads began in the 1980s. One popular example was Ken Blanchard's *One-Minute Manager*. But, as McGill observes, "Fads and fixes (like any prescription medicine these days) are expensive" (34). One must also add to these costs the cost of training and of taking time away from the job.

3. The Myth of the Megafirm

In this chapter McGill discusses the obvious but often ignored observation that small businesses are not like large businesses. In other words, methodology used by GE or Boeing may not be applicable to small firms (fewer than 20 employees).

4. The Myth of Entrepreneurial Management

The flat structure worked with 200 employees but not with 2000 employees. Small enterprises are lean by necessity, not by choice (63).

5. The Myths of Messianic and Managerial Leadership

"A leader is a leader because he leads as he leads because it is his nature to do so. Messiahs behave messianically" (88). "Common sense tells us that it is the followers who make the leader" (106).

6. The Myth of the Motivation Manager

One assumes that employee satisfaction is linked to performance (the assumption of motivation) (115). McGill cites examples of operators rushing to the next customer call by saying "Hello" and hanging up the phone. He also criticizes the importance of measurement by observing, "Whatever can be measured is likely to be inflated in importance and may displace energy from what workers really ought to be doing—whether or not it can be counted" (127). "The more ambiguous specific performance parameters are or the more difficult performance is to measure, the more style becomes a critical performance expectation" (143).

7. The Myth of the MBA

McGill sees the average MBA as having few people skills and too much theory and quantification.

8. The Myth of Technology

"The general agreed lesson from the GM experience is that new technology pays off only when coupled with changes in the way work is done" (189).

9. Managing without Myths

"The more we know to be involved in leadership, the less important the leader becomes" (204). McGill also writes about focusing on "small wins." A series of small wins is as important as, if not more important than, one big "win" that may be difficult to achieve. Managers need to be able to learn and listen. "Managing without myths means managing *with* employees" (214).

Pascale, Richard Tanner. *Managing on the Edge: How the Smartest Companies Use Conflict to Stay Ahead*. New York: Simon and Schuster, 1990.

Some of Pascale's observations that are recognized and observed by others, including the authors, are given here.

"Organizations have a tendency to do what they best know how to do; they are, if you will, the ultimate conservatives" (11). "Tools, techniques, and 'how-to' recipes won't do the job without a higher order, or 'hyper' concept, of management" (14). "The true path of insight, of course, required a study of both the sick and the healthy" (16). We fail to investigate failures. "The sobering truth is that our theories, models, and conventional wisdom combined appear no better at predicting an organization's ability to sustain itself than if we were to rely on random chance" (22).

The stronger elites are, the more difficult it is to achieve cross-functional teamwork (61). The market demanded that the company respond in ways that cut across functional compartments. "Success demands shorter response times" (63).

Companies must foster disequilibrium to ensure long-term survival (108). They must not favor stability but rather resiliency (the ability to absorb disturbances). Organizations must periodically step out of well-worn routines created and reinforced by past success (109). Significant changes occur in revolutionary ways (113).

Pearson, Karl. *The Grammar of Science*. 2nd ed. London: Adams and Charles Black, 1900.

This classic book contains one valuable piece of advice in its last few lines: "We must dare to be ignorant. Ignoramus, laboradum est" (531). Pearson believed that the scientific method can help us master any problem "however obscure and difficult it may at present appear. But we ought to remember what this mastery means; it does not denote an explanation of the routine of perception; it is solely the description of that routine in brief conceptual formulae. It is the historical resume, not the transcendental exegesis of final causes" (530–531). This quote leads to Pearson's observation about ignorance.

3

Human Resources Management, or the Preservation of Status Quo

Often, selectors are unable or unwilling to spend time analyzing the essential requirements of the job, and merely raise the qualification bar to simplify their task. However, this use of educational qualifications as a blanket measure of ability will not ensure the recruitment of the right people.

—Dominic Cooper and Ivan T. Robertson
The Psychology of Personnel Selection

The expression "human resource" is both unfortunate and often inaccurate. It is unfortunate because, as management guru Peter Drucker observed years ago, labor should be viewed as an added value and *not* as a resource to be mined or exploited. It is inaccurate because from the employees' point of view, the human resource department or staff rarely, if ever, represents their interests but instead represents the company's interests. And yet, despite Drucker's observation, when one looks at job advertisements, the perception that prospective employees are seen as resources to be mined from the vast pool of unemployed is easily understood.

It is our contention that one of the primary reasons why things remain more or less the same is that companies do not show much innovation when they interview and eventually hire people. This reluctance to take a small risk (when hiring individuals) implies that managers deliberately (or perhaps subconsciously) replicate jobs, thus guaranteeing a system that is in a perpetual state of equilibrium, a system where creativity or deviation from normal procedure is rarely encouraged—the very system that would reinforce the status quo partly responsible for the "always the same" syndrome.

The following observations are based on a six-month analysis of classified ads placed on three major Web sites. Our analysis was obviously not intended to cover all possible jobs, for such a task would have been well beyond our resources and ability. Instead, we focused on jobs relating to the quality profession in general in three western states: California, Washington, and Arizona. We searched for jobs using the keywords "quality manager" and "Six Sigma." These two keywords generated hundreds of job listings, usually about six to seven pages per search, and included postings for quality technician, quality analyst, quality manager/director, director of continuous improvement, Six Sigma Black Belt (and all related jobs, such as lean, Six Sigma, or Master Black Belt), process or continuous process improvement managers, directors, engineering jobs (particularly jobs relating to project management), and other similarly classified jobs.

Over the six-month period, approximately 500–600 ads were reviewed for content. Within the restricted selection of jobs as defined by our two keywords were basically two types: (1) managerial and (2) all other jobs (including engineering and nonengineering listings), which had no managerial responsibility. Each of these job categories had two types of descriptions: (1) a very long one and (2) a very short one. In the "very long description" category were jobs that included as many as 50 items (in the most extreme case) under the heading of "Responsibilities." For these jobs, the ideal candidate had to be some sort of superhuman capable of doing essentially just about everything from quality management to participating in design engineering, maintaining a health and safety program, ensuring that all environmental and quality regulations are in place, implementing or maintaining the current program, and much more.

The shorter descriptions were usually 10–15 lines long and, depending on the company, either very informative or vague as to the requirements. For the nonmanagerial jobs the *tendency* was to list very specific requirements. By specific requirements we are not referring to industry-specific requirements that invariably include a long list of acronyms supposedly understood only by the "specialist." We are instead referring to the practice of requiring, for example, knowledge of a specific software tool. We will refer to these jobs as *parts-replacement* jobs, because the impression one gets reading such job descriptions is that the employer is looking for a clone of the person who left—hence the idea that jobs are often perceived as parts with a specific part number. Whenever possible, companies will spend a considerable amount of time finding the right part that will fit precisely within a department.

In the case of Six Sigma (process improvement) type jobs, and also in many other similar jobs, the following words (or similar descriptions) are often used:

"Passionate about Six Sigma"

"Enthusiastically encouraging and educating all employees"

"Excellent communication and facilitation skills"

"Managing vision and purpose" (whatever that means)

"Establish a Six Sigma culture of continuous improvement"

"A can-do attitude"

"Desire to make a difference"

In other words, what these ads are telling us is that the current system is not working and is in need of a passionate, enthusiastic superhero who within a year, thanks to his or her can-do attitude and excellent communication and facilitating skills, will single-handedly encourage and educate all employees to establish a new culture that will transform the company and bring forth success and lasting happiness (at least for a year) to the executive management and eventually to the shareholders. The executive management, who is of course extremely busy, cannot possibly do all of that, but they will certainly support our hero for at least 12–18 months. If after this time results are not forthcoming or are below expectations, a new hero will obviously have to be found. Unfortunately, most managers do not recognize that unless they actively and tenaciously participate in implementing cultural change, nothing will ever happen! Hiring a superhero, if one can be found, will not change anything.

A desire to make a difference is certainly a personality trait well worth pursuing, but if it does not match with a commensurate authority to bring about change, it will be impossible for anyone to be successful in this pursuit. But even then, it will be difficult to bring about change, especially if the company in question has multiple geographic sites. It is well known that when members of a problem-solving team come from various geographic areas, it is more difficult to implement solutions, simply because the person in charge of the project finds it increasingly difficult to request changes to processes that are managed by others hundreds of miles away; such is human nature. Compounding the difficulty is that the very people who could/should intervene, namely, the upper-level managers, always appear to be too busy attending one more meeting or they simply believe that the very act of intervening or requesting change is not their responsibility. They can only assign tasks or responsibility or request more information (data), but they often do not act upon the information or take very long to react.

For smaller companies, where all activities are located in one geographic area, these types of problems (that is, inability to resolve problems) are minimized and should not occur. However, our hero will still have a difficult time going against the inertia (or resistance to change) characteristic of all organizations.

THE MYTH OF THE SUPERHERO

Michael T. Hannan and John Freeman (and others before them) recognized in their 1989 publication *Organizational Ecology* that organizations are much like an organism. Thus, they are limited in their "behavior" by the politico-socio-economic equivalent of ecological constraints.[21] In the first five chapters of their book,

---

21. Michael T. Hannan and John Freeman, *Organizational Ecology* (Cambridge, MA: Harvard University Press, 1989).

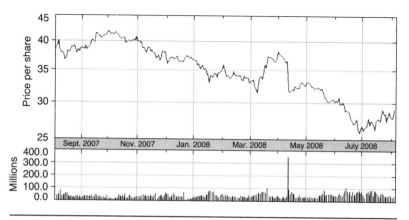

Figure 1   GE share value September 2007 to August 5, 2008.

Hannan and Freeman put forth some interesting observations that, based on our own observations, seem very pertinent to why things are likely to stay the same. Hannan and Freeman like to dismiss the myth that is all too often perpetuated in popular management books, that it is the actions of highly placed individuals (for example, CEOs such as the legendary Jack Welch at GE and Lee Iacocca at Chrysler) that helped guide companies to stellar success. As the authors so rightly point out, "The myths that develop around these people are magnified and romanticized by undisciplined retrospective analysis. We do not know how to answer whether the person makes the times, or whether the times make the person."[22] We believe that all too often it is the times that make the person; in other words, the person is in the right place at the right time. Looking at Figure 1, we see the value of a GE share steadily decline from approximately $40/share in late November 2007 to approximately $26/share in early July 2008.

Should we blame this $14 decline in share value on Jeffrey Immelt, current CEO of GE? Of course not. Such decline can, for the most part, be attributed to causes *outside* GE's control, namely the 2008–2009 recession in the United States and other countries. And yet, many management experts would likely attribute an

22.   Hannan and Freeman, *Organizational Ecology*, p. 40.

upward trend in share value to the impeccable leadership of the CEO. Naturally, such an explanation is equally invalid.

Hannan and Freeman point out that there are at least four factors that limit the capacity of managers (let alone the recently hired Six Sigma superhero mentioned earlier) to reshape an organization. The first factor is the organization's form, "which includes characteristics of the control system, the norms guiding behavior, and *incentives* used." The existing form constrains the choices available for any organization member, including managers. The second factor is scarcity of resources. "Scarcity," Hannan and Freeman observe, "makes adaptive change difficult to manage."[23] The remaining two factors include "pattern of competitions," which limits choice, and what has been referred to by many as "the limitations on rationality." The limits of rationality can be traced to (among others) Herbert Simon's 1947 doctoral dissertation (published as *Administrative Behavior*) and to political science with the 1959 publication by Charles Lindbloom entitled "The Science of Muddling Through."[24] This concept states that when faced with too much information, people and especially public administrators can use only a finite amount of information that leads to "good enough" solutions. Hannan and Freeman wisely observe that when one accounts for these factors, one must conclude that "managers do not matter much in accounting for variability in organizational properties."[25]

The authors go even further when they suggest later on in their book that contrary to mainstream thinking in organizational theory and research, "organizations rarely change

---

23. Hannan and Freeman, *Organizational Ecology*, p. 41 (emphasis added).

24. Charles Lindbloom, "The Science of Muddling Through," *Public Administration Review*, 19, no. 2 (1959): 79–88. For a biographical memoir on Herbert Simon, see http://www.apspub.com/proceedings/1472/213.pdf.

25. Hannan and Freeman, *Organizational Ecology*, p. 43.

their fundamental structural features." And in fact, in today's society, the *selection* in a population of organizations "favors forms with high reliability of performance and high levels of accountability."[26] Consequently, "to the extent that an organization comes to be valued for itself, changes in structural arrangements become moral and political rather than technical issues. Attempts at redesigning structures in organizations built on moral commitment are likely to spark bursts of collective opposition premised on moral claims in favor of the status quo. *Even if such opposition does not prevail, it delays change considerably.*"[27] From these observations, the authors conclude with the following interesting observation: "Resistance to structural change is a likely by-product of the ability to reproduce a structure with high fidelity: high levels of reproducibility of structure imply strong inertial pressures. . . . [and therefore] structural inertia can be a *consequence* of selection rather than a precondition."[28] In other words, as Herbert Simon observed well over 45 years ago: Selection tends to favor stable systems. And stable systems tend to be represented by large organizations that favor high inertia, resistance to structural change, and a culture promoted for the most part by international standards (for example, ISO

---

26. Hannan and Freeman, *Organizational Ecology*, pp. 69, 74.

27. Hannan and Freeman, *Organizational Ecology*, pp. 5, 7 (emphasis added).

28. Hannan and Freeman, *Organizational Ecology*, p. 77. Herbert Simon's quote is found on page 90. Forty-five years ago, the French sociologist Michel Crozier offered similar comments in his *Le phénomène bureaucratique* (Paris: Editions du Seuil, 1963, 1985). For example, Crozier observes that "a bureaucratic organization is an organization that cannot correct itself based on its errors" (229). Crozier goes on to suggest that bureaucratic organizations need a crisis to adapt and eventually reorganize themselves (243).

9001, AS9100) and a host of regulatory requirements that favor a documented procedural approach.[29]

CREDENTIALISM

A related problem, or rather a difficulty, is that of credentialism—or as Ronald Dore labeled it, the "diploma disease."[30] Credentialism probably originated in academia, where it became a requirement to have a PhD to teach in any university. Knowledge could be recognized only via the acquisition of a piece of paper that officially acknowledged that one had acquired some form of specialized, partly standardized (even esoteric) knowledge.

We are not suggesting that university degrees are not important; rather, we are referring to the certification mania perpetuated in part by state agencies that collect fees and by the diploma industry of various professional associations that clearly receive a healthy income for training seminars and certification programs.

---

29. Actually, things are a little more complicated than that because when companies talk about implementing changes they invariably mean that everyone will have to work harder, if not longer. Of course, the expression "working smarter" will often be mentioned. However, the end result is that you will have more to do and your projects have now become a burden. The majority of companies—at least in the United States—now expect people to absorb the task of solving problems in addition to performing their daily tasks. This additional responsibility can be very time consuming, especially when you have been assigned the task of saving your company a minimum of $500,000 per project and you have to work with a team of unmotivated coworkers.

30. Ronald Dore, *The Diploma Disease: Education, Qualification, and Development* (Berkeley: University of California Press, 1976). Today one could refer to the "certificate disease." The historian David F. Noble addresses a related issue in *Digital Diploma Mills: The Automation of Higher Education* (New York: Monthly Review Press, 2001). A summary of his book and many of his articles are published on the Internet, notably at http://communication.ucsd.edu/dl/ddm4.html and http://www.monthlyreview.org/books/excerpts/digitaldiplomamills2.php.

In particular, we are referring to the habit of most companies to automatically ask for certificates or other similar certification or credentials as a form of "approved knowledge." The focus on certificates is so strong that it has led to some irrational behavior whereby some human resource representatives or hiring managers do not know that someone with a bachelor's in statistics likely has more statistical expertise than someone who has received a certificate after attending a two-week course. Similarly, someone with a bachelor's in statistics and 10–15 years of experience in total quality management, which must invariably include some knowledge and expertise in problem solving, will be perceived as being *less* qualified than someone who went through a four-week course and might have two to three years experience. The words "Black Belt certification" seem to trump all other experience. We are well aware that these examples taken from the field of quality assurance occur in other professions, but we do not have the expertise to comment on these other areas. Unfortunately, the credentialism crisis is here to stay.

Some consequences of credentialism include:

1. Long courses and thick books or heavy binders designed by consultants. The heavier a set of binders, the more valuable they must be.

2. Expensive courses to justify the thick binders.

3. Learning the art of complicating the obvious, leading to a complex (elaborate) methodology to solve the easiest of problems that results in delays in solutions.

4. Standardized methodology indiscriminately applied to all problems.

5. The use of signs everywhere in a plant to label the obvious. Signs, particularly directional or safety/hazard signs, are unquestionably valuable and even necessary. But when signs are used to tell you that you are entering such and such an area, that you can store sugar in such and such a cabinet, or that "this is a drug-free zone," one should question the value of such compulsive labeling.

One of the authors once saw a senior director in charge of continuous improvement and 6S label six identical red bicycles used in a warehouse. The senior director then proceeded to delineate and label six areas—this in a futile, if not wasteful, attempt to ensure that each duly numbered bicycle would be placed in its correct location.[31]

6. A proliferation of acronyms or specialized jargon that is in part responsible for the abuses of verbal intelligence.

All these consequences are conducive to yet another unfortunate corporate disease: functional myopia.

FUNCTIONAL MYOPIA: A SIDE EFFECT OF TOO MUCH TRAINING OR INAPPROPRIATE EXPERIENCE

Researchers have shown that the acquisition of an extensive verbal vocabulary may in fact lead to what some authors refer to as functional myopia.[32] *Functional myopia* is a condition whereby your view of a problem or a particular situation is hampered by your training or experience in a discipline. This myopic condition is acquired, for example, by anyone who persists in applying one and only one set of tools to solve problems.

Functional myopia is characterized by the following symptoms:

1. The tendency to analyze or otherwise formulate all problems (or perceive any situation) in terms of one or two

---

31. We recognize that these comments will likely offend fans of 6S principles. We do not question the value of 6S but rather its indiscriminate and, at times, senseless application.

32. Dietrich Dorner, *The Logic of Failure* (Cambridge, MA: Perseus Books, 1996).

particular tools or techniques or even methodology or perspective. By extension, one could also suggest that functional myopia has some deeper influences. Indeed, we have already observed that it is not uncommon for managers to believe that only people with the right vocabulary (specific to a methodology) can perform specific tasks. The problem with this mistaken perception is that all too often the "new" vocabulary is nothing more than a rephrasing of an ancient concept. Thus, for example, instead of talking about Takt time (an old concept developed in the 1940s), one must now know about 3P (which is very similar to Takt time). Instead of talking about failure modes and effects analysis (FMEA)—an old risk analysis type technique used on processes or a design to identify, for example, an inadequate design— one must now refer to PFMEA, the redundant abbreviation that stands for process failure modes and effects analysis. Countless other examples could be given. We do not wish to imply that one should not employ these useful techniques (when in the proper context); we simply want to point out that in many cases, the forced use of certain (all too often recycled) techniques may actually get in the way of solving some problems or resolving some simple issue.

2. The tendency to apply the last successful technique to solve any subsequent problem. If a series of diagrams was found to be useful for a particular problem (for example, boxplots), inexperienced problem solvers assume that the same set of diagrams should be helpful for most other problems. Naturally, these assumptions are based on false premises induced by a mild case of functional myopia and can often lead to frustration.

3. The tendency to overcomplicate the solution to the simplest of problems. This includes the inability to simply look at the data; that is, look at the numbers. A corollary to this problem is the need to find the appropriate

statistical technique(s), supposedly required to analyze the data, without even first looking at the numbers. We would like to suggest that often the answer to a problem can be found by simply "reading" the data.

4. The inability to distinguish between the types of problems or, stated differently, the tendency to treat all problems as if they are of the same type when in fact they are not.

Other manifestations of functional myopia often attributable to extensive but limited experience have been observed.

NOT EVERY FACTORY IS A NUCLEAR PLANT!

Many years ago one of the authors conducted a quality management system audit of a rope factory. The team consisted of the author and another auditor, who had many years of experience auditing nuclear plants. It soon became clear to the author that the second auditor was auditing the rope factory as if it were a nuclear plant. People tend to apply their previous work experience to any new work environment whether or not it is appropriate. Thus, a person with experience in manufacturing Class III heart stents for the medical industry will want to implement the same rules and procedures when working for a toothbrush distributor. Invariably, the final argument presented by the new hire to convince his coworkers to adopt his or her solution or "improvement" sounds something like this: "When I used to work at XYZ medical this is what we did." What these good-intentioned people forget is that the manufacturing context is different—a manufacturer of highly regulated Class III devices is *not* the same as a toothbrush distributor. This should be obvious, and yet it is almost always forgotten.

CONTEXT IS VERY IMPORTANT
WHEN FACED WITH A PROBLEM

We now come to the all-important question of corrective actions and the paperwork they tend to generate. In the world of quality assurance, whenever a defect occurs, the accepted practice is to generate a corrective action to permanently fix the problem (also generally referred to as finding the root cause). This approach is certainly reasonable, but as the following real-life example demonstrates, it is not reasonable in all cases.

A distributor of various healthcare products ships three to four million units per year across the United States and Canada. After three years of operations the distributor received a customer complaint because hair was found in an electric toothbrush (the product retailed for about $120). The incident immediately generated a corrective-preventive action to address the problem. The proposed solution was to require all workers to wear hairnets. Was the solution appropriate to the risk associated with the perceived problem? Over a period of three years the distributor would have shipped 12–16 million units. The sole customer complaint generated over that period of time is equivalent to a defect rate of 1 in approximately 12 million (assuming the most conservative scenario)—a rather impressive performance even in the world of Six Sigma, where three to four defects per million is considered a major achievement. Is it reasonable, then, to implement a procedure that requires every one of the 100 assembly line workers to wear a hairnet?[33] Would a cost-benefit analysis have concluded such a solution to be cost effective or even necessary? Was the issuance of a corrective action in this particular case even necessary?

This inability to assess risk and apply appropriate corrective action is evident in many industries. A one-in-a-million-years event in a nuclear plant could very well have drastic consequences for millions of people, but a one-in-twelve-million event that involves a $120 healthcare item that might occur once every three years is a very different story. Similarly, the argument that it is imperative to have a desk well organized with all documents and files clearly labeled is often presented by 6S and procedure

---

33. One process engineer decided to go further and required that anyone with a beard had to also use a beard net.

aficionados. The standard argument for having an impeccable desk is as follows: "If Johnson is absent and we receive a phone call from one of our customers asking for a specific document or piece of information that we know should be available on Johnson's desk, anyone should be able to easily access the necessary information." When presented with such an argument, usually all present nod in agreement and promise to maintain a spotless, well-organized desk (a 6S desk). Although the reader may have sensed that one of the authors' desks (which one?) is rarely spotless, the following question could still be asked: What are the odds that a customer would ask for the said information on precisely the day that Johnson is absent? Since there are 200 working days in the year, the odds that someone will call exactly on the day Johnson is absent (two mutually exclusive events) are 1/200 × 1/200, or 1/400, or 0.25 percent, a low probability indeed. But even if such a rare event should occur, what is wrong with simply saying, "Mr. Johnson will be back tomorrow"? After all, that is precisely what people used to say before 6S came along and told us that such an answer was no longer acceptable. It's all about context.[34]

No wonder that with such scenarios it has become increasingly difficult for some companies to rapidly adapt or react to situations and move forward. Worse yet, when things get a little complicated, we can always rely on planning to save the day. Or can we?

---

34. We are aware that many international, national, and/or regional regulations or standards require companies to implement a multitude of (often) costly procedures. Although some of these regulations are of dubious value to society, they certainly do benefit the regulatory agencies and their associated bureaucracies that have been mandated the task of monitoring industries (see, for example, Philip K. Howard, *The Death of Common Sense: How Law Is Suffocating America* [New York: Random House, 1994]).

Annotated Bibliography

Berg, Ivar. *Education and Jobs: The Great Training Robbery.* New York: Praeger Publishers, 1972.

Berg demonstrates that people with more education are not necessarily more productive. However, they are more likely to be frustrated with their work and eventually quit and find another job (because they are not challenged). In other words, the data show that people tend to be in jobs that utilize less education than they have. But this has not prevented companies from continuously asking for more education.

"If education is a formal credential of progressively less economic importance, a more serious question arises than whether the most educated people in our society are 'utilized' in some economically meaningful way" (60).

Berg is wise enough to present five interpretations of the data.

"We found that educational achievement was inversely related to performance thus conceived" (87), thus disproving the myth associating education with productivity. However, education "may well be relevant to the 'promotion potential' of workers in a shop or plant where title and pay changes reflect differences in job tasks and obligations" (90). Better-educated people get ahead by changing jobs, whereas their less educated peers move into the higher-paying jobs vacated by employee turnover (91).

"To argue that well-educated people will automatically boost efficiency, improve organizations, and so on may be to misunderstand in a fundamental way the nature of American education, which functions to an important, indeed depressing, extent as a licensing agency" (104).

Thus by "training robbery," Berg means that the return on investment is not always worth it, especially for the teacher. Indeed, as educators get more education, they are less likely to want to continue as teachers (181–182).

Castellan, N. John, Jr. (ed.). *Individual and Group Decision Making.* Hillsdale, NJ: Lawrence Erlbaum Associates, 1993.

In Chapter 6, "Decision Errors Made by Individuals and Groups," author R. Scott Tindale concludes that groups do not always check errors. "In fact, under certain circumstances, groups make more errors, or more extreme errors, than individuals. The question then becomes why do groups make less errors on problem-solving tasks yet make more errors (at least some of the time) on decision-making tasks" (121).

Cohen, William A. *A Class with Drucker: The Lost Lessons of the World's Greatest Management Teacher.* New York: AMACOM, 2008.

This book is a good summary of Drucker's philosophy. We learn that Drucker had very little managerial experience, but he was a good listener and probably a good interviewer. From Frederick Herzberg, *The Motivation to Work* (New York: John Wiley & Sons, 1959), we learn that money is not sufficient to motivate workers (223). Workers must be led, not managed (good advice). Don't use Theory X. Motivate each worker according to the individual and the situation (good) and "treat all workers as if they were volunteers, because they are" (230). Drucker saw labor as an added value and *not* as a resource (214) (as in human resource, the term implies that it can be exploited until completely used). In "What Everybody Knows Is Frequently Wrong" (Chapter 3), Cohen explains that common knowledge is often based on erroneous assumptions. Decision makers must look at the reliability and validity of the data (getting to the core); this is a valuable observation, particularly as it relates to databases.

Connolly, Kathleen Groll, and Paul M. Connolly. *Competing for Employees.* Lexington, MA: Lexington Books, 1991.

An interesting combination of marketing and human resources is developed in the book. The supplier-customer relationship is extended to employee-employer.

"Contrary to what some may believe, good morale does not always lead to positive motivation. Positive motivation does not always lead to high productivity" (35).

"Satisfied employees are not always effective and effective employees are not always satisfied. Morale is thus not a sure road to improved productivity. While positive morale makes management easier, it is not directly linked to effective performance" (36). Few employees respond to cheerleading.

The authors offer a good review on how not to write a job ad. Often, human resource people write ads that can turn off good candidates (64). This observation is still true today.

Most people leave jobs because the job offers no challenge (advancement and pay are the next two reasons). The authors do not mention that companies occasionally encourage their employees to leave. Such techniques are used when companies do not want to provide a severance package. Demotion is a common technique, along with assigning unjustified blame.

"Yet much recruiting reflects company-centered thinking. This is unfortunate because the applicant's first meeting with a company is often in such communications, whether in print, through a recruiter, or other means. In truth, company-centered communications can lead to the wrong people applying for your positions" (62). The authors review a couple of newspaper ads that ask for a lot of responsibilities for a job that pays very little. This trend of piling up responsibilities for less and less salary reemerged in the United States during the 2008–2009 recession.

Cooper, Dominic, and Ivan T. Robertson. *The Psychology of Personnel Selection*. New York: Routledge, 1995.

The book opens with an interesting quote from Peter Herriot, who forecast in the 1980s that companies in the 1990s would "fail to recruit and retain the people they need to help them change. People make the place, and people set the pace" (1). The quotation also appears in Herriot's *Recruitment in the Nineties* (London: IPM, 1989), p. 1.

"Often, selectors are unable or unwilling to spend time analyzing the essential requirements of the job, and merely raise the qualification bar to simplify their task. However, this use of educational qualifications as a blanket measure of ability will not ensure the recruitment of the right people" (2).

Studies in the 1980s (meta-studies) "showed that for many of the personnel selection methods, when there is good correspondence between the job and person specifications and the measuring instruments used, predictions are reasonably accurate" (3). Unfortunately, "successive surveys regarding the use of selection methods indicate that most companies rely on the classic trio—application blanks, ad hoc interviews and reference checks—which are among the least reliable and valid selection methods" (4).

Dore, Ronald. *The Diploma Disease: Education, Qualification, and Development*. Berkeley: University of California Press, 1976.

This is an interesting book. We have included it because of its criticism of credentialism.

"Everywhere, in Britain as in India, in Russia as in Venezuela, schooling is more often qualification-earning schooling than it was in 1920, or even in 1950. And more qualification-earning is mere qualification-earning—ritualistic, tedious, suffused with anxiety and boredom, destructive of curiosity and imagination; in short, anti-educational" (ix).

"My thesis may not be entirely popular. It rests on the assumption that good (as opposed to qualified) administrators and doctors and teachers are, if not exactly born rather than made, at least pretty well made by their early teens, and that in the process of perfecting them after that, formal schooling may be as much a hindrance as a help" (xi).

Dore describes the process of educational inflation whereby a bus company starts employing "senior certificate leavers" as conductors (5). "Or it might just be that, faced with fifty applicants for five bus conducting jobs, all of whom could do the job equally well, it just simplifies the whole process to consider only the ten people with senior certificates—and provide a clear objective and legitimate reason for saying no to the other forty" (5).

Qualification escalation leads to certificate devaluation. "Most of the developing countries are still at the Victorian rote-learning stage, but gradually they will grow out of it" (7). Dore refers to the process of schooling for qualification (as opposed to education) as credentialism or "credentialing."

The problem with this system of qualification is that "the would-be employee has learned to take orders, not initiatives" (11). "They [employees] will have learned the virtues of punctuality, regularity, hard work, conformity to regulation, obedience to the instructions of superiors. These are not insignificant qualities, perhaps. But are they the qualities most required in the members of administrative and managerial bureaucracies given the task of modernizing their society? What of imagination, creativity, honesty, curiosity and the determination to get to the bottom of things, the desire to do a good job for its own sake? These are not qualities likely to be bred by a prolonged dose of qualification-oriented schooling—most prolonged in those highest up in the hierarchy on whose initiative the most depends" (11–12).

Dore has a great sense of humor and is very perceptive. He uses a quote from the World Bank regarding a new strategy for schooling: "Do not be put off by the heavy weight of Unospeak, the high adjective/noun ratio, the liberal spattering with 'comprehensive', 'integrated', 'coherent', 'well-meaning'; the penchant for the word 'system' (though still, luckily, only 'learning systems', not yet 'learning experience delivery systems'). Underneath it all there are good intentions, generous impulses and a lot of sense" (105).

Graig, Robert L., and Lester R. Bittel (eds.). *Training and Development Handbook*. American Society for Training and Development. New York: McGraw-Hill, 1967.

According to Donald L. Kirkpatrick, in the chapter "Evaluation of Training," there are four steps to evaluating training (87–112):

1. Reaction: How well did conferees like the program?
2. Learning: What principles, facts, and techniques were learned?

3. Behavior: What changes in job behavior resulted from the program?

4. Results: What were the tangible results of the program in terms of reduced cost, improved quality, etc?

When the reactions to a training session are found to be very good, the evaluation measurement has just begun (95). "It is important to recognize that favorable reaction to a program does not assure learning" (96). We all have attended lectures where the speaker's presentation is well accepted by the group but where a "careful analysis of the subject content would reveal that he said practically nothing of value—but he did very well" (96).

Hochschild, Arlie Russell. *The Managed Heart: Commercialization of Human Feelings.* Berkeley: University of California Press, 1983.

Hochschild focuses on the airline industry and flight attendants. Although the following quotation refers to flight attendants, it is equally valid for training in general.

"The fact that their training manuals are prepared for them and that they are not themselves entirely free to 'tell it like it is' only illustrates again how deskilling is the outcome of specialization and standardization" (120).

McGregor, Douglas. *The Human Side of Enterprise.* New York: McGraw-Hill, 1960.

This is an excellent book that should be read by all managers and human resource professionals (others would also certainly like this book). The following summary does not do justice to the wisdom found within the pages of McGregor's book.

"The acquisition of knowledge is a fairly straightforward process provided the individual wants the new knowledge" (208). "It is the elaboration, and particularly the standardization, of this process for large numbers of people which lessens its value. It is all too easy for higher-level management or staff groups to decide for others what they need in the way of additional knowledge. Courses and programs are then prepared and offered" (208–209).

"The learning is limited because the motivation is low. Moreover, this strategy soon generates negative attitudes toward training in general and thus hampers the creation of an organizational climate conducive to growth" (209). "Above all, it is necessary to recognize that knowledge cannot be pumped into beings the way grease is forced into a fitting on a machine. The individual may learn; he is not taught. Effective education is always a process of influence by integration and self-control" (211).

Motivation is often low. McGregor's point is still relevant today with the Six Sigma or any other training scheduled by some manager. People are expected to "volunteer" (210). He also warns of the expectation of seeing an immediate return for the education (typical in Six Sigma programs). This is a case of measuring the wrong thing, McGregor says (213). The purpose of university courses (which he favors) is not to provide answers to problems "or tricks of the trade. It is to broaden the manager's understanding of his job, to challenge some of his preconceptions, to make him better able to learn from experience" (215).

McGregor recognizes that groups must have certain characteristics in order to be effective; one characteristic is that there must be disagreement and no one group member can impose his or her will. There must also be lots of discussion, and people must listen (232–234).

Robbins, Harvey, and Michael Finley. *Why Teams Don't Work: What Went Wrong and How to Make It Right*. Princeton, NJ: Peterson's/Pacesetter Books, 1995.

This is a pretty good book with some ideas about what can go wrong with teams and how to fix problems. The authors recognize that not everything can be solved with teams (good!). They also criticize many of the myths about teams. "Manuals become the fiefdom of certain, otherwise powerless, centralized functions, like personnel. The departments occasionally make a religion out of the big book, because it is all they have" (48).

Rynes, Sara L. "Recruitment, Job Choice, and Post-hire Consequences: A Call for New Research Directions." In *Handbook of Industrial and Organizational Psychologists,* Vol. 1, edited by Marvin Dunnette and Leaetta Hough, pp. 399–444. Palo Alto, CA: Consulting Psychologists Press, 1994.

"On the practitioners' side, descriptive research has revealed that recruiters are largely untrained, recruitment sources largely unevaluated, and costs and benefits of recruitment practices largely unknown . . . and only one of 105 respondents noted a need for additional recruitment research" (439–440).

Shulman, Beth. *The Betrayal of Work*. New York: The New Press, 2003.

The following quotation is very pertinent to some of the issues presented here in our chapter on human resources: "Skills have been defined in terms of educational level or technical expertise, generally related to the ability to use computers. But this notion overlooks the types of skills possessed by child-care workers, nursing home workers, or hotel workers—skills of patience, caring, conscientiousness, and communication" (107).

Zerfoss, Lester F. "Use of Consultants." In *Training and Development Handbook*, American Society for Training and Development, edited by Robert L. Graig and Lester R. Bittel, pp. 428–439. New York: McGraw-Hill, 1967.

The following observation regarding consultants and training was made more than 40 years ago, and yet it is still very relevant today, proving once again that the more things change the more they remain the same.

"These pseudo-consultants often appear as 'package' salesmen with a service or product which looks good superficially, provides a general 'busy work' program that is strong on promises, and almost invariably ends with no real accomplishment. Since these packages are apt to ride the training fads of the moment, exploit the latest gadgets or training aids, and are skillfully and dramatically promoted, even sophisticated managements are attracted to their siren songs" (429). Scott Adams has said the same in his cartoons.

4

The Limits of Plans
and Planning

In planning we don't do anything; we just consider what we might do.

—Dietrich Dorner
The Logic of Failure

Planning may not be effective at assessing the future, but it can be a good way to assess the present.

—Richard Farson
Management of the Absurd: Paradoxes in Leadership

There are probably as many quotations about the virtues of planning as there are about the absurdity of some planning. One of our favorite quotations about planning is attributed to the great philosopher Immanuel Kant, who made the following observation more than 200 years ago:

Making plans is often the occupation of an opulent and boastful mind, which thus obtains the reputation of a creative genius by demanding what it cannot itself supply, by censuring what it cannot improve, and by proposing what it knows not where to find.[35]

---

35. Immanuel Kant, quoted in Dietrich Dorner, *The Logic of Failure* (Cambridge, MA: Perseus Books, 1996), pp. 176–177.

It is difficult to improve on such a wise observation, and yet although many well-known business analysts have proposed similar arguments over the years (see annotated bibliography), the quest for project planning and the more elusive strategic planning is still with us and is not likely to disappear soon. Which company will be brave enough and innovative enough to accept the challenge to eliminate strategic planning or at least reduce its importance?

Although Henry Gantt is generally credited with inventing Gantt charts, it was Karol Adamiecki (1866–1933) who, using what he called harmonograms, first introduced the concept of project planning as early as 1896. There is little doubt that the preparation of PERT plans and Gantt charts is highly advisable for very large and complex projects where the timely delivery of supplies (by numerous suppliers) and completion of critical phases are crucial to the successful on-budget and on-time completion of a project. Our objection to planning is not aimed at such applications but rather at the obsessive requirement imposed by many managers to prepare a plan for any and all projects, including the simplest set of activities. In particular, we find it absurd to attempt to predict and plan to the week which activities will be completed and when—this, even when the series of planned activities has never been attempted before.

THE PARADOX OF PLANNING

The paradox of plans is that when you know how to perform a task (or a series of tasks), you do not need to plan to execute a set of actions for a successful on-time completion. Do you prepare a plan for inviting a few friends over for a barbecue? Beyond planning the time and place for the barbecue, there really is no need to prepare a plan for when the steaks will be grilled, how long it will take to cook them, when the salad will be prepared, and so on. You simply know when to start and how long it will take. Of course, planning a barbecue is not as complex as designing and manufacturing an airplane or a ship or completing a huge government contract, and it's certainly not as costly when deliveries are late. In such cases, plans are valuable, but they will not prevent delays. But then again, the problem with planning is that managers (or perhaps it is the software tools they like to use) treat every process or project as if it were a gigantic government project.

Before you can start on anything, even an activity you have never performed before, you are invariably required to prepare a plan outlining how and when specific tasks will be completed. It is difficult to comprehend the logic of such a request, because anyone with common sense will tell you that it is impossible to plan the future and equally impossible to plan for something you have never attempted before. And yet, that is exactly what is required of many people every day throughout the world. Of course, these plans are meaningless and full of inaccuracies or errors, which explains why plans are invariably in a perpetual state of revision. Yet, once printed, "the plan," which can be upward of 90 percent guesswork, is viewed as the official road map. All activities and performances, including, for example, the infamous "percent completion" metric, will be measured vis-à-vis the plan. Deviation from unreasonable (estimated) dates will have to be explained. Your inability to satisfy a purely whimsical goal or target will be questioned, and you will even be asked if you need help to come up with a better plan. Absurdity will rule, and unless you comply with the request for a plan, you will be perceived as the odd man or woman. Worse, if you do not satisfy the irrational schedule imposed by the plan, you may well be transferred to another job or even terminated.

The following account helps illustrate what can happen when organizations prepare plans for activities they have never before undertaken. In a move to consolidate its resources, Company A decided to shut down several of its sites and transfer its assembly lines to Company B. Although Company B had much experience with such transfers and had even worked with Company A in the past, this transfer was more complex in nature and was therefore a totally new experience for Company B's management. To complicate things further, Company A had either never before been involved with such a transfer or appeared to have little experience with such transfers. The final twist to this odd scenario was that Company A had been working with its processes for several years—processes that were well established and mature. Despite these facts, Company A demanded that the transfer of material and knowledge, as well as the implementation of a complex quality and environmental system, be completed within 10–12 weeks. In other words, Company B had to write procedures, be trained on the new procedures, learn how to operate three new software systems, implement two management systems, and be fully operational within 12 weeks, an insanely aggressive schedule. To mitigate any potential difficulties, a very detailed plan was prepared by someone (probably a consultant). The plan, created in the comfort of an office using a well-known software application, consisted of the obligatory precise timelines specifying to the day when each of a long series of tasks would be completed. Viewed on a 20-inch computer monitor, the meticulous-looking plan no doubt appeared masterful and easily achievable. Of course, the plan, or rather the planner, did not anticipate the possibilities of Black Swans (discussed in the section "Planning Risk in a World of Black Swans"); this option is not available on any software application. Consequently, when unexpected difficulties began to occur, it became evident that it would be impossible to satisfy certain delivery dates. Rather than admit that the problem was with its plan, Company A (the customer) began blaming Company B for not adhering to the plan that, for some inexplicable reason, was approved by Company B. Not wanting to offend Company A, Company B reacted by putting more people on the project. Although one could reasonably argue that the inadequate allocation of resources played a part in the ensuing scheduling problem, this was certainly not the root cause. Confusion or perhaps an unfortunate unwillingness to react to such an absurdly aggressive timeline was in fact the real problem; adding more people to the project at this late stage did not really help alleviate the problem. It should be pointed out that the so-called transfer of knowledge could have easily been achieved in about five to six weeks, but both companies would have had to recognize that another approach could have been used. Unfortunately, faced with yet another case of functional myopia, both parties failed to recognize this second option.

As we shall now see, the absurdity of planning can find its apogee when companies spend countless frantic hours preparing strategic hoshin plans.

THE HOSHIN PLANNING TOOLS (THE VERY ESSENCE OF COMPLEXITY AND ILLUSIONARY CONTROL)

Hoshin planning tools tend to be very costly software packages, and the more costly they are the more controlling they are. Anyone using these software tools spends a considerable amount of time answering questions supposedly designed by experts who decided that unless you precisely follow each step in the proper sequence, you will not logically achieve your goals. Therefore, when an isolated individual at corporate headquarters decides to invest hundreds of thousands of dollars buying these gargantuan software tools, *everyone* is required to use them, as this is the dictate from those above. And since they are at the top of the hierarchy, they must know more than the people below them. Unfortunately, the foundation for these planning tools is built on weak assumptions. Enormous structures of goals, metrics, completion dates, milestones, and so on, are built into these *estimates* that appear to be accurate only because they are reproduced on a computer screen.

Naturally, the assumption is that the tool is correctly used, but all too often this is not the case. Since one does not have time to learn all the subtleties of such an elaborate tool, one learns by doing and invariably runs the risk of making fundamental mistakes. These mistakes may have a very costly impact on the company (and eventually people) because if errors are made and the plan has been approved, it is practically impossible to backtrack and correct these erroneous estimates; thus, the errors are now part of the official plan by which all activities and performances will be measured.

Although we don't go into great detail about hoshin plans, a brief description is nonetheless required. Anyone wishing to learn more can easily obtain information on the Internet by simply searching for "hoshin." We would hasten to add that if your company does not yet use hoshin, you should perhaps avoid trying to use such tools. If, however, you choose to use hoshin, be sure to use it properly and, more important, wisely, so as not to become prisoner of a software package.

What Is a Hoshin Plan?

The following propaganda-sounding explanation of hoshin planning does not begin to explain the complexity of the process, but we present it here nevertheless (key concepts are in italic):

Hoshin planning is an *annual hierarchical planning* and execution process that *brings focus, alignment, discipline, and rigor* to the achievement of breakthrough objectives in an organization. Typically an organization will focus on one or two breakthroughs that are critical to the *long-term strategic objectives*. The breakthrough and associated target become the *objective and target* of the hoshin plan. A set of *long-term strategic objectives* is developed to ensure achievement of the top-level objective.

As the plan cascades down the organization in a series of discussions and planning sessions, each strategy on one level becomes an objective at the next level down, and the process of developing a supporting set of necessary and sufficient strategies for each new objective continues. At some point in the deployment, usually *between one and three levels down,* the plan switches *to implementation tables.* These tables detail the set of tasks to be executed across the organization that together will achieve the breakthrough. It is easy to see that with, for example, six strategies supporting the top-level objectives and a further six substrategies supporting each of these top objectives, we have 36 linked strategies with possibly 10 tactics, each supposedly aligned and planned to deliver the top objective(s). Such plans, we are told, are not undertaken lightly, however. *When deployed and executed with discipline* [reminiscent of the military approach favored by the Whiz Kids at Ford], they serve to focus, empower, and energize the organization around a significant goal. Plan-based hoshin can help you succeed [succeed in what, we are not told].

The suggestion that plan-based hoshin can help you succeed is open for debate. The problems with hoshin planning are many. The key concepts emphasized in the definition help show why hoshin planning is difficult to implement correctly, but they do not tell us why. We are told that hoshin planning is:

> *Annual hierarchical planning* that *brings focus, alignment, discipline, and rigor* to the *long-term strategic objectives*. It consists of *the long-term strategic objectives* that *cascade down the organization in a series of discussions and planning sessions*. We are also told that this cascading down can reach *between one and three levels down*. The *switch to implementation tables . . . , when deployed and executed with discipline*, can help a company succeed.

The fundamental problem with hoshin planning is that it is based on the illusionary assumption that *strategic planning* or any planning (long or short) is possible. And yet, as has already been noted by illustrious philosophers over 200 years ago and more recently by well-known business researchers and analysts such as Henry Mintzberg, planning for organizational strategies is difficult at best: "[Since] organizational strategies cannot be created by the logic used to assemble automobiles . . . planning may have less to do with strategy making than is often claimed."[36] Moreover, the "all things being equal or remaining the same" assumptions

---

36. Henry Mintzberg, *The Rise and Fall of Strategic Planning* (New York: The Free Press, 1990), pp. 13, 29.

inherent in any plan (hoshin or otherwise) could not have antici-
pated the colossal collapse of the financial world and all of its
repercussions. As the recent financial crisis and world recession
have amply demonstrated, no amount of "new" planning, especially long-term planning, can anticipate future crises. And yet,
such plans continue to be generated.

The cascading effect mentioned in the definition is one of the
most troublesome characteristics of hoshin planning. Contrary
to what is stated in the definition, the "discussions and planning
sessions" (between management and the people responsible for
the implementation of these targets and objectives at various
lower levels) are rarely, if ever, conducted. Worse yet, managers
who are invariably under pressure to demonstrate financial performance impose unreasonable targets and/or objectives that
can be only partially met (see "The Case of the $3.7 Million War-
ranty Reduction" in Chapter 6). Unfortunately, partial success
(even of unreasonable goals) is all too often viewed as failure
that requires a corrective action, one that invariably leads to a
reorganization or a search for a more "performing" personnel
(see Chapter 2).

These difficulties are also due to the fact that these tedious
and time-consuming hoshin plans are implemented without
proper training, acts that can have disastrous consequences. Managers lacking discipline and rigor often set unreasonable goals
that, once entered into the plan, must be defended no matter how
irrational the original objectives/goals were. These classic mistakes, observed decades ago by W. Edwards Deming, continue to
this day. Consequently, instead of first "seeing" what a process or
series of processes is capable of, many managers will arbitrarily
set targets and then expect the process(es) to achieve these targets
in an arbitrary period of time, only to be later disappointed when
their staff does not achieve the target.

Unfortunately, it can take two to three years before a company
finally realizes that such complex, elaborate, and detailed plans
are for the most part (especially if not used properly) a waste of
time and resources.

PLANNING RISK IN A WORLD OF BLACK SWANS

Planning risk has always seemed to us to be an oxymoron. You can analyze risk, as the insurance industry does to assess rates, but this assumes that you have a database that allows you to calculate probabilities. Otherwise, you can make wild—or at best, educated—estimates upon which complex scenarios are based. We are not claiming that all risk analyses are a waste of time, as we do recognize that the task of anticipating possible scenarios or disasters (as practiced, for example, in FEMA) and developing solutions to these scenarios is well worth the exercise. But one must also recognize that in the absence of hard data, these scenarios often either flirt with fiction or cannot anticipate unusual conditions.

In recent years, particularly since 2000, risk analysis has become so popular that it is mentioned in many job descriptions and has become in many industries an absolute requirement. And yet, risk analysis is another element of the "always the same" syndrome. When one reads about the virtues of risk analysis, one is left with the impression that this methodology, built for the most part on estimates or guesses, is essential for just about any business activity. The problem with risk analysis is that most people who talk about it fail to recognize what financial analyst Nassim Taleb refers to as the Black Swan factor. A Black Swan, Taleb explains, is an outlier that carries an extreme impact and, "in spite of its outlier status, human nature makes us concoct explanations for its occurrence *after* the fact, making it explainable and predictable."[37] Taleb observes, "Our inability to predict in environments subject to the Black Swan, coupled with a general lack of the awareness of this state of affairs, means that certain professionals, while believing they are experts, are

---

37. Nassim Taleb, *The Black Swan: The Impact of the Highly Improbable* (New York: Random House, 2007), pp. xvi, xvii.

in fact not."[38] Consequently, Taleb concludes, "The problem with experts is that they do not know what they do not know."[39]

Taleb's argument, known to anyone who has performed extensive data analyses, is that although many events are normally distributed and predictable, life-changing events behave more like Black Swans. They are not normally distributed but instead follow highly skewed distributions, are highly unexpected, and have an enormous impact, as the financial world found out in late 2008.

Annotated Bibliography

Ackhoff, Russell L. *The Democratic Corporation*. New York: Oxford University Press, 1994.

Summary of Chapter 3, "Quality of Work Life and Its Products."

"Those who so define quality (i.e., as meeting or exceeding the expectations of customers) usually assume that the customers are the same as the consumers. However, this is often not the case—for example, where a supplier sells a product to a wholesaler who sells it on to a retailer who sells it to someone who may give it as a gift to another" (92). "Total quality should apply to the expectations of all those who are affected by what an organization does, all its stakeholders" (93).

"Improvement programs should be directed at getting what people want, not, as is usually the case, at getting rid of what they do not want" (98). Ackhoff then talks about idealized designs, which are designs that start with the assumption that the thing to be improved was destroyed last night. Ackhoff also recognizes

---

38. Taleb, *Black Swan*, p. xx.

39. Taleb, *Black Swan*, p. 147. These lines were written approximately four weeks before a series of major financial collapses occurred on Wall Street in September and October 2008. Some economists, such as Dr. Ravi Batra of Southern Methodist University, have long written about the problem of free trade and laissez-faire capitalism. As early as 1990, Dr. Batra wrote against government policy that favored an unregulated financial market; for more information, visit http://ravibatra.com.

that creative but discontinuous improvements are usually worth much more than a string of small but continuous improvements (99). Idealized designs allow for the removal of many self-imposed constraints and free the mind to be creative.

Regarding planning backward from the present, Ackhoff suggests that it is better to plan from "where one wants to be right now to where one is right now" (101). His argument doesn't seem to be very convincing until he offers the following observation: "The reason for this (advantage in thinking backward from where we are) is that most of the obstructions between us and where we want to be are in our minds, not 'out there,' in others or the environment. When we look to where we want to be from where we are, we tend to project self-imposed constraints on external sources that are out of our control" (103). We can more effectively deal with the future by "either increasing our control of it or by making assumptions about the rest, preparing contingency plans based on these assumptions" (102).

On total quality management (TQM), Ackhoff notes that it raises "some issues it is not equipped to handle. For example, it tries to change management's activity from supervision, control of the actions of subordinates, to leadership, guiding their interactions and encouraging and facilitating their development. But it provides no theory to guide managers in efforts to create organizational structures that facilitate the management of interactions and the development of subordinates" (105). Circular organizations, according to Ackhoff, are the answer.

The following quotation is still very contemporary: "The trouble is, as we grow up, we don't allow ourselves enough space for not knowing. As life goes on, we increasingly live in our perception of what's 'right,' 'wrong,' 'impossible,' etc. instead of in what's real" (264).

Bernstein, Peter L. *Against the Gods: The Remarkable Story of Risk*. New York: John Wiley & Sons, 1998.

This is an excellent book that includes many historical references.

"The essence of risk management lies in maximizing the areas where we have some control over the outcome while minimizing the areas where we have absolutely no control over the outcome and the linkage between effect and cause is hidden from us" (197).

The following anonymous quotation about information is even more relevant today:

> The information you have is not the information you want.
>
> The information you want is not the information you need.
>
> The information you need is not the information you can obtain.
>
> The information you can obtain costs more than you want to pay. (202)

Bernstein relates an amusing story about the economist Kenneth Arrow. When Arrow was asked to forecast the weather for several days, he realized that the long-range forecast was no better than numbers pulled out of a hat. When he reported the results to his superior, he was told, "The Commanding General is well aware the forecasts are no good. However, he needs them for planning purposes" (203). Reducing uncertainty is a costly business.

Bernstein also reviews Tversky and Kanehman's prospect theory, which states that people are influenced by the degree of belief (coined by Keynes) rather than rational decision. People have problems recognizing how much information is enough and how much is too much. Reference points are very important to the decision-making process (how rich you are is *not* as important as how much richer or poorer you will be based on your decision) (274). Too much information may distort decisions. "People will bet on vague beliefs in situations where they feel especially competent or knowledgeable, but they prefer to bet on chance when they do not" (281). In other words, people are not rational.

Past data (historical data) provide us only with one sample of the economy and the capital markets, not with thousands of separate and randomly distributed numbers (335). This observation is also valid with databases; historical data can be valuable, but one must not forget the context.

Dorner, Dietrich. *The Logic of Failure.* Cambridge, MA: Perseus Books, 1996.

This excellent book covers several major topics including problem solving, training, and planning. Some of the author's valuable comments on planning are summarized here.

Dorner quotes Moltke on strategic thinking (Mintzberg may not be aware of Moltke) when he states that one must constantly adapt action to context: "Everything is in flux, and we must adapt accordingly" (98). Bad participants, Dorner observes, tend to act first before gathering information (the reverse of good participants). "The less information gathered, the greater the readiness to act. And vice versa" (101).

"In planning we don't *do* anything; we just consider what we *might do*" (153). Detail planning . . . is a waste of time. As Napoleon said, "One jumps into the fray, then figures out what to do next!" (161). A redundancy of potential command (many advisers) can lead a general to lose a battle because of too much expert advice (161).

Insecurity leads to precise planning and greater insecurity and more imprecise planning (164). "Bad problem solvers use 'absolute' concepts that do not admit to other possibilities or circumstances" (175).

"Making plans is often the occupation of an opulent and boastful mind, which thus obtains the reputation of a creative genius by demanding what it cannot itself supply, by censuring what it cannot improve, and by proposing what it knows not where to find"—Immanuel Kant (176–177).

Douglas, Mary, and Aaron Wildavsky. *Risk and Culture: An Essay on the Selections of Technical and Environmental Dangers.* Los Angeles: University of California Press, 1982.

While this is a difficult book to read, the following quotation is worth citing: "Once the idea is accepted that people select their awareness of certain dangers to conform with a specific way of life, it follows that people who adhere to different forms of social organization are disposed to take (and avoid) different kinds of risk. To alter risk selection and risk perception, then, would depend on changing the social organization" (9).

Gigerenzer, Gerd. *Calculated Risks: How to Know When Numbers Deceive You.* **New York: Simon & Schuster, 2002.**

This is an interesting book on the subjects of mechanical rationality and inferential statistics versus intuitive statistics.

Howard, Philip K. *The Death of Common Sense: How Law Is Suffocating America.* **New York: Random House, 1994.**

This book, written by a lawyer, is a must-read for anyone interested in learning about the absurdity of many of the rules and regulations of the Occupational Safety and Health Administration (OSHA), the Food and Drug Administration (FDA), the Environmental Protection Agency (EPA), and other regulatory agencies.

Meyer, Marshall W., and Lynne G. Zucker. *Permanently Failing Organizations.* **Newbury Park, CA: Sage Publications, 1989.**

The authors argue that, over time, organizations tend toward sustained low performance. The participation of multiple actors "whose interests sometimes correspond but sometimes conflict, poses significant problems for the ability of owners . . . to impose anything approaching rational utility maximization upon organizations" (22–23).

To the question, why cannot interests be easily aligned in organizations around performance? the authors suggest, "Most people are more concerned with maintaining existing organizations than with maximizing organizational performance" (23). When performance is high, the interests of workers and management (that is, those wishing to meet official objectives [for example, profit]) correspond. "However, should exogenous events cause performance to deteriorate, which occurs sooner or later in most organizations, then the interests of those seeking to maintain organizations of those seeking high performance become antagonistic, sometimes dramatically so" (23).

Mintzberg, Henry. *The Nature of Managerial Work*. New York: Harper and Row, 1973.

This is one of the earliest books that describe the daily activities, constant interruptions, and work fragmentation experienced by managers.

Mintzberg, Henry. *The Rise and Fall of Strategic Planning*. New York: The Free Press, 1990.

"Organizational strategies cannot be created by the logic used to assemble automobiles" (13), and Mintzberg adds, "planning may have less to do with strategy making than is often claimed" (29).

"An organization can plan (consider its future) without engaging in planning (formal procedure) even if it produces plans (explicit intentions); alternately, an organization can engage in planning (formalized procedure) yet not plan (consider its future); and planners may do all or some of these things, sometimes none of them" (32).

"Planning reduces flexibility and is fundamentally a conservative process: it acts to conserve the basic orientation of the organization, specifically its existing categories" (175).

"Planning relies on formal techniques of forecasting to look into the future, and the evidence is that none of these can predict discontinuous changes in the environment" (182). Flexible planning is an oxymoron (184).

"An obsession with control leads to . . . an aversion to risk, which means a reluctance to consider truly creative ideas and truly quantum changes, both of whose effects are unpredictable and so beyond formal planning" (203). Mintzberg also speaks of "the pronouncement of platitudes" that consume time but achieve nothing (216).

Strategy, Mintzberg observes, is always about stability in an organization's behavior (239). Serious changes in strategy generally mean a shift in gestalt, a new conception (240).

Mintzberg also notes that the problems with hard data are that (1) they are limited in scope and often do not encompass noneconomic and nonquantitative factors, (2) they are often too aggregated for effective use in strategic making, (3) they arrive too late to be used in strategy making, and (4) they are often unreliable (258–264).

Later, Mintzberg suggests that managers must use their tacit knowledge and be intuitive (269).

The problem with formal planning is that it only deals with the consequences of strategy but does not create strategy (330). Some authors (for example, Khandwalla) have found a strong negative correlation between planning and the growth rate of a company (343).

Mintzberg, Henry, Bruce Ahlstrand, and Joseph Lampel.
Strategy Safari: A Guided Tour through the Wilds of Strategic Management. **New York: The Free Press, 1998.**

The authors review and criticize the limitations of nine strategic schools: Design, Planning, Entrepreneurial, Cognitive, Learning, Power, Cultural, Environmental, and Configuration.

Mintzberg is aware of the limitations of hard information when he notes that it is difficult to substitute the information obtained from the expression on a customer's face (69). Also, Mintzberg suggests, don't rely too much on expert MIS systems. A single story from a disgruntled customer can be worth a lot more than reams of market research (71; we could not agree more). The authors also criticize benchmarking, which they call "the herding effect" (119).

The authors also provide a nice review of the Honda case that shows that Honda penetrated the U.S. motorcycle market by accident (the company was almost forced into it) and not through a strategic analysis of the market. The same could be said of the cell phone, which was originally designed for a very different purpose than its current use.

The story about the bees and flies in a bottle is an interesting anecdote. Mintzberg et al. explain that the bees are more intelligent, but it is the flies that get out of the bottle. Why? Because they flutter "widely hither and thither" (178).

Singleton, W. T., and Jan Hovden (eds.). *Risk and Decisions.* New York: John Wiley & Sons, 1987 (republished in 1994).

Emil Spjotvoll, in "Probability: Interpretation and Estimation," explains quoting W. D. Rowe's *The Anatomy of Risk*, that risk estimation involves several steps (13):

- The probability of the occurrence of a hazardous event
- The probabilities of the outcomes of this event
- The probability of exposure to the outcomes
- The probabilities of "consequences"

Objective vs. subjective probabilities: One method to assess subjective probabilities is to use the Delphi method, where the final estimate is the geometric mean of failure rates estimated by experts, possibly weighted by how "expert" an expert is (21).

Berndt Brehmer (Chapter 2, "The Psychology of Risk") points out, "We do not perceive risks, we perceive various features of decision problems and this, in turn, leads to a feeling of risk. Consequently, it makes little or no sense to ask whether risk is correctly perceived. All we can do is to compare intuitive risk estimates with risk estimates that have been obtained from various formulae" (26).

Perceived risk differs from expert judgment about risk. "Expert judgment often focuses upon fatality rates but this is only one of the aspects that affects perceived risk and therefore perceived risk does not always agree with the risk computed by engineers." Laypeople and engineers look at different things (36). When designing systems, engineers look at objective risks, and the general public uses subjective risk perception.

Jens Rasmussen, in the chapter "Risk and Information Processing," explains that "most human choice is not, however, based on such rational analysis which is mainly typical of formal professional activities, but on holistic, intuitive and mostly subconscious judgments" (111). This would involve the ability to "predict the behavior of the system and to compare with the intended performance" (116).

Alan Hedge, in the chapter "Major Hazards and Behavior," mentions studies that classify risks along four or more dimensions: whether the risk is natural or manufactured, whether the associated event is ordinary or catastrophic, whether exposure to this is voluntary or involuntary, and whether its impact is immediate or delayed (142).

Stacey, Ralph D. *Managing the Unknowable: Strategic Boundaries between Order and Chaos in Organizations.* San Francisco: Jossey-Bass Publishers, 1999.

The author repeats what others have said. Nonetheless, a few interesting quotations regarding strategic planning and other topics are provided for the benefit of the reader.

"The key to success lies in the creative activity of making new maps, not in imitative following and refining existing ones" (1). Stacey seems to discover that no one knows what the long term can bring and therefore planning is of little value (he refers to plans and vision as "fantasies": "forming visions and making assumptions are not realistic possibilities" (7). Moreover, one individual cannot be in control of an organization.

Stacey confirms by stating that there is "no connection between strategic planning and performance" (26). However, he does question the idea that companies that "adapt to their environment" are successful (31). "Long-term plans serve only as a rational defense against the anxiety provoked by great uncertainty. Visions and shared values are mystic versions of the same defense. The new perspective leads us to abandon these defenses and focus our attention instead on improving the learning and political interaction that constitute real strategic management" (42).

Taleb, Nassim Nicholas. *The Black Swan: The Impact of the Highly Improbable.* New York: Random House, 2007.

Taleb's book is frightfully prophetic. It was published a year before the financial meltdown of Wall Street in September 2008, which required unprecedented government intervention. What is particularly disturbing is that Taleb found that there are financial advisors and economists who, he states, don't know anything about risk or prediction, and he is very critical of these individuals. It would appear that Mr. Taleb was absolutely right.

5

Technology and the Age of Unnecessary Complexity

The trouble with "how to" books and biographies of famous executives may be that they tantalize us with tips to make us more successful, and distract us from our own possibilities. What's missing in these "how to" books and biographies is that people who really make things happen are standing in a different place.

—Russell Ackhoff
The Democratic Corporation

Younger generations of managers but also older managers infatuated with the use of software cannot seem to solve or do anything without the help of what is generally referred to as *software tools*. We doubt that we will be able to change this trend. However, we hope to demonstrate how software tools often get in the way of solving problems and render the task more tedious; in some cases the software tool may not even help us solve anything.

The problems associated with software tools and databases are many and include the following:

1. "Analysis paralysis," a condition caused by overly controlling software tools that can delay solution to relatively simple problems for months.

2. Databases not designed to solve most problems but rather to keep accountants or auditors busy and happy, and/or errors in databases that lead to wasted time and costly errors.

3. The curse of unending data slicing made easy by the excessive use of the features of Microsoft Excel's Pivot-Tables, to name but one example.

4. The availability of too much statistical power (or sophistication) that leads to an excessive amount of time spent analyzing and reanalyzing data that often are of limited value or even irrelevant. We should also mention the unfortunate habit of some individuals, including managers, of wanting to reduce everything (no matter how complex or how simple) to a Pareto chart. These charts are certainly very valuable, but they are not always appropriate.

We will briefly review each of these issues.

SOFTWARE TOOLS THAT GET IN THE WAY OF SOLVING PROBLEMS

The primary problem with software tools (we will not talk about engineering simulation software or design software) is that they are often designed to control the way you think and/or the way you approach or analyze a problem.

Let us begin by reviewing the case of the company that wanted to use a pricey software tool designed by a consulting firm to manage problem-solving projects.

A large multinational company that one of the authors has worked with decided that in order to better manage all of its (worldwide) problem-solving projects, it would use a sophisticated and very expensive software package. Although the decision process leading to the purchase of the software was not known, several managers close to the decision felt, with some justification, that the software would allow the company to centralize all of its projects in a vast depository that could be used as a learning or teaching database for others. However, rather than allow each division to use the software as it saw fit, corporate headquarters decided that one group in charge of corporate training would ensure that the software *was used properly*. This idea to centralize the decision-making process was probably not a good idea. What was wrong with the software?

The author was asked to review the software, which shall henceforth be referred to as SX. The fundamental problems with SX were numerous and typical of many systems that attempt to "behave" as expert systems, whereby decision rules supposedly developed by experts attempt to guide and control a user through a particular methodology. In Six Sigma jargon, the methodology is known as the DMAIC process. (Note: SX is not, strictly speaking, an expert system of the type used to diagnose problems or specific medical conditions.) Some of the unfortunate characteristics of SX were the following:

1. The DMAIC software module that was designed to completely control the user's thinking process made it extremely tedious to use.

2. The user had to answer all questions within a particular phase *before* being able to move to the next phase.

3. It could take up to an hour to complete some phases.

4. When the user had completed the process, someone not involved with the project would review the entries to ensure that the user had properly completed all of the phases.

The process of using the software correctly had become the ultimate hurdle in proving that one had successfully completed a project. In fact, for some relatively easy (short) projects, the time required to answer all the questions almost equaled the time it took to complete the project. The software package did not allow the user to answer "not applicable," because the consultants who designed the package had arbitrarily decided that every project, regardless of complexity, had to go though all the phases as defined by the high-price consulting firm. Complexity had taken over.

Although the recommendation to not use the software was predictably ignored, the author has since learned that a little over a year after the suggestion was made, the use of SX was dropped as a requirement to complete projects.

LIMITATIONS OF DATABASES

Twenty years ago, Bruce Baird wrote the following:

> Most "management information systems," although originally designed for the purpose of informing, do not achieve this objective. They merely inundate the administrator with data. Information may be contained somewhere in the system, but is often hidden among mountains of data, thus discouraging search and encouraging reliance upon opinions and intuition. This "data overload/information shortage" problem is a common one for the modern executive. Although the reasons are diverse, one major cause of the problem is that designers of most management information systems are not the users of the system. When one group designs the system and another group uses the output of the system, a natural tendency develops that encourages increasing the quantity and complexity of pages, numbers, and frequency of reporting rather than the *quality* of information necessary for decision making.[40]

Baird concluded by remarking that the solution lies in cooperation and communication between the system developers and the system users. The object is not to generate n reports of x pages each produced every y days.

Information should be:

1. Reliable (different people should get the same results)
2. Timely

---

40. Bruce F. Baird, *Managerial Decisions under Uncertainty* (New York: John Wiley & Sons, 1989), p. 235.

3. Economical (the cost of information is not greater than its value)

4. Necessary (no extraneous or irrelevant material)

5. Sufficient (the maximum amount of uncertainty has been removed)

6. Accurate (free from error)

7. Usable

To achieve these "somewhat inconsistent" objectives, decision makers must analyze tradeoffs in the objectives' characteristics.[41]

And yet, despite these wise comments, companies all over the world continue to repeat the mistakes outlined by Baird. Databases designed for one specific purpose (often related to some accounting need) are tapped daily to try to extract information needed to solve unrelated problems. The authors have been involved in many cases where data analysts spent upward of 20–30 hours to extract a simple table of data required for a particular analysis. To make matters worse, once the data were collected and analyzed (another two to four hours of analysis), it was discovered that they were not what was needed and the whole process had to be repeated. The reason why the results were wrong (or misinterpreted) was that the variables that were analyzed were not clearly defined, which led to a misinterpretation of the results. Such problems can have serious consequences when the (erroneous) analysis is presented to management and wrong decisions are made, leading to more errors and additional costs.

---

41. Baird, *Managerial Decisions under Uncertainty*, p. 236. Similar reproaches have been made in certain pricey enterprise resource planning software applications derogatorily known in some circles as "Slow and Painful." Often poorly implemented or not used properly or to their fullest potential, these mammoth software applications have also been known (perhaps unjustly) to negate or conflict with principles of lean management.

Case Study I: Estimated Time to Repair— What Everybody Knows Is Frequently Wrong

The estimated time to repair (ETTR) was one of a dozen metrics monitored by the customer service department of a large multinational company. When a customer important to the company complained that a field service engineer (FSE) took three days to show up at his site, management became alarmed and immediately requested an investigation (without verifying with field service the validity of the customer's claim or the nature of the complaint). A preliminary analysis that relied on the use of a database revealed that over a period of several months, the *average* ETTR was a little over two days, which was unacceptable. Based on this analysis, it was decided that a questionnaire would be designed and sent to all FSEs (something that had never been done before). A brief statement was included at the beginning of the survey explaining that in view of the fact that the ETTR was more than two days, a survey had been initiated to find the root causes for such a delay. Many of the FSEs who replied pointed out that they could not believe the two-day average ETTR value. Indeed, their responses indicated that, on average, FSEs responded to calls within three hours. How could the discrepancy be explained?

It turned out that the FSEs had a different definition of ETTR. To them the ETTR was reasonably understood to mean the time it would take for an FSE to reply to a call once a call was received from the Technical Center. However, as far as the customer was concerned, the ETTR was the time that elapsed from the moment the customer completed the call to the Technical Center, where all calls are first answered, to the time the FSE showed up at the site. In other words, the time it took for the technical support group to call an FSE was not "seen" by the FSE. Moreover, the technical support procedure required that the person receiving the call had to first try to solve the problem. If after four hours the problem could not be resolved by phone, an FSE would then be sent to the site.

In addition, all calls placed around 3 p.m. West Coast time (6 p.m. East Coast time) would be received by the FSE the *next day*, thus automatically adding 12–15 hours to the response time. Consequently, although the FSEs were indeed responding to a Technical Center call within two to three hours, they did not know that some calls were received 12–15 hours earlier. Therefore, 12–15 hours plus 3 hours = 15–18 hours minimum, or a day and a half—which is very close to what the initial analysis revealed. Unfortunately, the metric did not account for such intricacies. Maybe this was the correct approach, because from the customer's point of view, the wait time was often upward of 18 hours, or closer to two days (on average), before the customer actually saw an FSE. It was not always this way. A year prior to the reported event, the average response time was almost 50 percent faster. What had gone wrong?

As investigators began to dig into the problem, the reason why the average ETTR had steadily gone up over the past 12–15 months became clear. In a spirit of cost saving, a high-level manager had decided to cut overtime pay for FSEs. Consequently, whereas FSEs had been able to visit clients until the early evening hours (6:00 p.m.–7:00 p.m.), they could no longer do so. All the work that remained unfinished by 5:00 p.m. had to be resumed the following day.

In addition, many FSEs questioned the need to have a centralized call center. Many customers had also complained about the quality of the phone service. And yet, despite these findings and the suggestions from FSEs, including a detailed report presented to upper management, nothing was ever done, because it was not *politically suitable* to implement the proposed solutions. To this day, the ETTR is still the same and may even have gone up. More of the same.

PIVOT TABLES: CUTTING *n*TH DIMENSIONAL DATA CUBES FOREVER AND EVER

One of the unfortunate side effects of large databases is that they contain a vast array of variables from which all sorts of information can be obtained, some of which may even be pertinent to the problem to be solved. Let us assume that you have access to a database that collects information on, say, a modest 20 variables. Let us further assume that out of these 20 variables you are interested in only 6. Combinatorial statistics tells us that there are 56 ways to analyze various combinations of these six variables. In other words, with only six variables to analyze, you could end up producing as many as 56 tables. The ability to slice data matrices with software using such features as PivotTables (in Microsoft Excel), for example, allows the data to be "filtered" and thus produces vast arrays of tables. Imagine the volume of tables if you have to look at 10 variables.[42]

---

42. You can perform all the calculations by visiting http://www.mathsis fun.com/combinatorics/combinations-permutations-calculator.html.

Flooded by the amount of information provided by these tables, most people cannot digest what they see and either delay their conclusion or try to collect more data to conduct more analyses. This is not the only paradox faced by analysts using increasingly powerful software tools.

STATISTICAL SOFTWARE WITH TOO MUCH POWER

Over the past 30–35 years, using statistical software has become increasingly easy. But along with ease of use has come increased statistical power, available at the click of a button. Novice data analysts are now able to perform sophisticated analyses, regardless of whether the analysis is justified or even valid. At the opposite end of the spectrum are individuals who believe that after four weeks of training they are now statisticians who can perform the most advanced statistical analysis on any data, regardless of whether the analysis is needed or pertinent to the problem at hand. As a result, we now have an army of expert problem solvers who spend an inordinate amount of time trying to use various (and likely inappropriate) techniques. Projects drag on forever and may take six to eight months to conclude, whereas six to eight weeks would have been enough if only the statistics did not get in the way of the solution.

POOR ORGANIZATION AND PRESENTATION OF INFORMATION

Many people do not know how to present data, and the use of software tools will not facilitate the task. We have already briefly alluded to the fact that many individuals, including experienced managers, like to use color charts (in some cases, three-dimensional color charts) when a simple table would be more useful. Presenting information to an audience is not an easy task, and some fundamental errors can easily be avoided. We have often seen managers produce charts without dates. For example, a chart depicting a trend on a particular metric would indicate only first quarter, second quarter, and so forth, on its abscissa. The chart's title would not even indicate what month or period the data cover. This is important information; one needs to know the time period covered by any chart.

Another unfortunate habit people have when reporting data is that all too often they present the data in percentages instead of actual raw numbers. A couple of examples will help illustrate our point. We once saw a metric reported as "percent of engineering deviations closed within 15 days." This awkward definition could have been avoided by simply preparing a histogram of how long it takes (in days) to close a deviation, an approach that would have been much more informative. And instead of reporting "percent on-time delivery," it would be more useful to measure and report the number of days that installations are late. A histogram of these data would be more informative than a percentage, and moreover, the histogram would also have a percentage for each frequency. Reporting the data as they are collected is usually the better approach, but alas, too many people are set on reporting a diluted version of the original data—and it would appear that percentages are here to stay (for a while anyway).

CONCLUSION

Can we conclude that statistical software tools have helped us solve problems more rapidly than our predecessors solved problems 30, 40, or even 60 years ago? We doubt it. Similar observations could be made with planning software tools, corrective action or audit software tools, SAP software, MRBII software, or any other software that provides the average user much more power than he or she will ever use or have time to use—too busy, too many meetings, too many reports to prepare, too much data to analyze (sound familiar?). One of the authors, who has some 12 years of experience as a quality system auditor, has seen some very poor software tools used by very large companies to schedule and monitor their internal audit program. First developed in the mid-1990s as a result of the ISO 9001 movement, these programs were written by programmers who had never conducted an audit. The resulting product is an exceedingly tedious application that complicates the simplest audit by emphasizing control rather than performance.

When software tools are used to implement antiquated concepts of quality management, irrationality reaches its apogee. An example includes the use of software tools to conduct acceptance sampling.[43] Acceptance sampling has been around for almost 80 years, and in this age of ISO 9001, Lean-Six Sigma, or the other latest and greatest alphabet soup methodology, it is surprising to see this technique still being used (all too often wrongly). The misapplication of acceptance sampling in the United States alone must cost companies and their vendors millions of dollars. Although a whole chapter could be devoted to this topic, we will limit our comments to a couple of observations:

1. Quality engineers often set the acceptance criteria too tight and without really knowing the agreed-upon acceptance quality level (AQL) of the supplier. We have also noticed that when lots are accepted month after month, no one thinks of relaxing the criteria to shift to a skip-lot acceptance or to even stop inspection. Such a logical conclusion cannot be reached, because the software "tells us to inspect."

2. Another important factor all too often ignored is the cost of sampling and testing associated with the item being inspected. One of the authors once observed a quality engineer reject a lot of approximately 500 cardboards because 4, costing a total of $12, had a minor visual defect. The cost of filling out the paperwork to reject the lot and then wait for a likely deviation far exceeded the $12 by

---

43. *Acceptance sampling* is a field of statistical control that consists of taking a sample from a lot of delivered raw material (or components) and measuring one or more quality characteristics. With the information obtained from the sample, a decision is made to either accept or reject the entire lot. A vast literature is available on acceptance sampling, including, of course, the Internet.

at least a factor of 15–20. If the cost of inspection is larger than the cost of the part being inspected and/or the cost of the problem incurred by a defective part, one should seriously consider receiving lots without inspection.

When using a software application to control the process of acceptance sampling, one sacrifices flexibility and rational reasoning to automated mindless procedures dictated by the rigorous application of the acceptance plan.

An unfortunate consequence of software tools is that it is their inherent nature to consume huge amounts of data in order to spew an endless number of reports that may or may not be read. Since someone must enter these data and perhaps even read the reports and/or tables, software tools, like most other technological inventions, demand much of people's time and energy. Similarly, when a company refuses to modernize its software and persists in using 25-year-old software (that is on its nth revision), inefficiencies are bound to occur. We are not blaming the software but rather the software industry (which over the years has skillfully managed to overcomplicate issues) and those managers who are convinced of the value of such complex systems or who refuse (no doubt for lack of time) to correctly implement or use the software or to properly or adequately train the people who will use the software.

Annotated Bibliography

There are many works on the effects of technology on society and the work environment in general. For some early and classic contributions, see Jacques Ellul, *The Technological Society* (New York: Vintage Books, 1964) and *The Technological Bluff* (Grand Rapids, MI: William B. Eerdmans Publishing, 1990).

Kawasaki, Guy. *Rules for Revolutionaries*. With Michele Moreno. New York: Harper Business, 1999.

The book's main theme is on innovation and the marketing of new products and services. One of the interesting concepts proposed by Kawasaki, who used to work with Apple Computer, is what he refers to as "evangelism." A company should search for customers who not only are buyers of its products or services but also believe so much in the product that they "convert" others about the virtues of the product.

Pink, Daniel. *A Whole New Mind*. New York: Riverhead Books, 2005.

With a simple and direct language, the author covers the six senses that must be developed to see solutions in a different way. Some of the themes Pink explores include design, empathy, and technology.

Tenner, Edward. *Why Things Bite Back: Technology and the Revenge of Unintended Consequences*. New York: Random House, 1997.

Even though this book was published in 1997, Chapter 9, "The Computerized Office: Productivity Puzzle," is still very pertinent, as it illustrates that spreadsheets of data do not help managers reach better decisions. One of the important references Tenner cites is the work of Peter G. Sassone, whose research showed that "computerization has helped reduce rather than promote the amount of time that (managers and professional) employees spend performing their highest and best work" (265). As Tenner concludes Chapter 9 he wisely observes that "bugs, glitches, and crashes have a positive side: they are the machine's way of telling us to diversify our attention, not to put all of our virtual eggs in one electronic basket" (267)

On the limitations of PowerPoint presentations and other related topics, see the work of Edward Tufte, http://www.edwardtufte.com/tufte.

6

Problem Solving: Still a Problem!

To state a problem properly is not to suppose it solved in advance.

—André Gide
The Immoralist

Some of the most popular problem-solving and creativity techniques were proposed over 55 years ago by Alex Osborn in his 1953 best seller, *Applied Imagination*.[44] And yet, even as far back as 1953, problem solving was certainly not new. Indeed, Osborn, who coined the term "brainstorming" in 1939, cites numerous articles on problem solving dating as far back as the early 1920s. It would seem that 80 years of contemplation would have resolved every possible issue of problem solving, but that is not the case.

As Peter Drucker once noted, one must approach problems with your ignorance, not one's expertise. This is wise advice, particularly when one is dealing with wicked problems.[45]

---

44. Alex Osborn, *Applied Imagination* (New York: Charles Scribner's Sons, 1953).

45. One should also observe that companies tend to ignore this advice when hiring people. Most companies believe they need experts with a well-defined range of expertise to help them solve a variety of problems.

WHAT ARE WICKED PROBLEMS?

It has been argued that the single cause of the "too many meet-ings" complaint is that companies are all too often confronted with the difficult task of trying to resolve societal or policy prob-lems—in other words, the very types of problems Horst Rittel and Melvin Webber describe in their 1973 paper as *wicked prob-lems*, as opposed to "tame problems."[46]

The following story will help set the stage for describing wicked problems. One of the authors lives in Southern California, an area known for its arid climate and perennial droughts. After too many years of below-average rainfall (which in Southern Cal-ifornia is only 25–30 centimeters per year or less) and continued increased population (well over 20 million people in Southern California alone), the many water districts responsible for pro-viding water to Southern California residents have begun to issue voluntary water conservation warnings. Given that the price of water increases every year and that Southern Californians are encouraged to conserve water, it is not uncommon to see lawns with many brown spots. Of course, lawns (which consume much water) are not a logical choice for landscaping in arid Southern California, but that is another story.

In the community where the author lives, there are many retired people who have nothing better to do than to walk around the community to ensure that all the front lawns are green and properly watered. In early July 2008, the author was told by a nice gentleman that the grass in his front lawn was not green enough and that he should increase the watering or perhaps treat the lawn with some chemicals to eliminate what appeared to be a fungus that turns lawns an unpleasant brown color. Now, if you had been assigned the task of solving this problem, how would you proceed? You could, of course, treat the lawn for a possible fungus and/or increase watering, but what if that is not the

---

46. The original article from Horst Rittel and Melvin Webber can be found at http://www.uctc.net/mwebber/Rittel+Webber+Dilemmas+General_Theory_of_Planning.pdf.

problem? Is there a solution for this wicked problem, whereby two opposite requests are competing for a solution? On the one hand, the water district wants residents to cut down on their water consumption, and on the other hand the home association wants owners to increase their lawn watering to prevent ugly and esthetically unpleasant brown spots. A wicked problem is born. The only solutions, which are both rather costly, would be to remove the grass and replace it with a more environmentally friendly plant cover (in other words, semi-arid plants like cacti) or remove all plants and introduce a rock landscape. Of course, one could ignore the problem and delay the solution, which is precisely what many problem-solving teams and politicians who have to deal with many wicked problems often do.

Rittel and Webber define a wicked problem as being a problem with the following criteria:

1. It consists of an evolving and interlocking set of issues and constraints that make it impossible to clearly formulate a problem statement. In essence, you don't really understand the problem until you somehow stumble upon (in the word of Herbert Simon) a "satisficing" less than optimal solution.

2. There are, as is often the case with many problem-solving projects, many stakeholders who have an interest (sometimes even conflicting interests) in how the problem should be resolved. This transforms the problem-solving process into a politico-social event whereby getting the right answer is not as important as finding a diplomatic and likely suboptimal solution that will be acceptable to all.

3. The constraints on the solution that are often characterized in terms of limited available resources change over time. The classic scenario in problem-solving teams is that members are pulled out of a team by management to solve supposedly more important issues. Another scenario is that the rules by which the problem must be solved are changed. Examples of rule changes include

(1) a change in expected savings (for example, instead of committing to an initial savings of $1 million, management now expects $3 million), (2) changes in the timeline, which are usually reflected in a reduction of time, and (3) changes in commitment (for example, management no longer supports the project).

Because there is not a definite, well-stated problem, the solution is forever delayed and the problem-solving process ends because the team runs out of time (money), interest, or energy.[47]

When faced with wicked problems, it is not unusual for decision makers, particularly politicians, to muddle through a solution.[48] Recognizing that policy problems that involve multiple interested parties can never be solved comprehensively, Charles Lindbloom proposed that instead of achieving a *rational efficient* solution, decision makers must sometimes gradually arrive (also known as *gradualism*) at a solution using a series of incremental steps (known as *incrementalism*); in essence, one slowly converges to a satisfying solution by using an iterative process.

The need to muddle through solutions has not been recognized by problem-solving methodologies. This methodology assumes that all problems can be rationally solved once all interested parties have been identified and the DMAIC process (the favored process of Six Sigma teams) is put in place. However, as Lindbloom demonstrates, such a rationalistic approach to problem solving is not always possible.[49]

---

47. A summary of wicked problems can be found in a Web article published by E. Jeffrey Conklin and William Weil, "Wicked Problems: Naming the Pain in Organizations," http://www.leanconstruction. org/pdf/wicked.pdf.

48. Charles Lindbloom suggested the expression "muddling through" in his classic 1959 article, "The Science of Muddling Through," *Public Administration Review* 19, no. 2 (1959): 79–88.

49. Readers interested in bounded rationality should see Herbert Simon, "Bounded Rationality and Organizational Learning," *Organizational Science* 2, no. 1 (1991): 125–134, and James March, *A Primer on Decision Making: How Decisions Happen* (New York: The Free Press, 1994).

Case Study II: The Case of the $3.7 Million Warranty Cost Reduction

High-level managers in the medical division of a multinational company became alarmed when they learned that the warranty cost of various scanners had recently climbed from an average of slightly under 4 percent in 2004 to almost 11 percent in mid-2006 (see Figure 2). Management wanted to know what had caused an increase of almost 7 percent. To answer this question, they assigned two individuals to analyze the problem. One of the individuals recently graduated from the company's training course, and the other individual was a Six Sigma Master Black Belt. Their task was to reduce the warranty cost level back to 4 percent or less within a year.

Within a day of being informed of the assignment, the Master Black Belt tried to explain to management that this was not a reasonable project for a newly trained Black Belt, even if that person was under the supervision of a Master Black Belt. The $3.7 million warranty cost reduction expected by management was unreasonable, especially because the reduction had to be achieved within a year. The

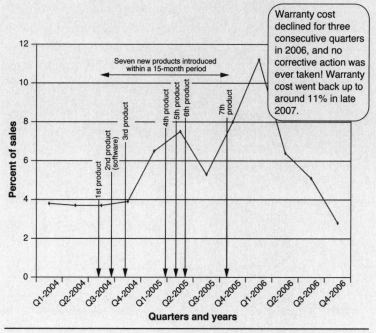

Figure 2　Warranty cost 2004–2006.

project definition was very broad and involved at least four departments located across the country and included many suppliers. Despite the warnings, management went ahead with the project and formally included it as one of its major strategic objectives for the year. The project's proposed savings (somewhat arbitrarily defined by management) were the largest of all projects defined for that year.

After a 10-month investigation that produced well over 500 pages of analysis, the following conclusions regarding warranty cost were reached:

1. From late 2004 to late 2005, seven *new* products had been introduced (see Figure 2). Consequently, comparing 2004 warranty costs (averaging about 3.8 percent) for a couple of mature products reaching the end of their life cycle with 2005 warranty costs (averaging between 6.5 and 7.5 percent) for *seven new products* was not only unrealistic but wrong. When it was suggested that warranty costs would eventually come down, management ignored that statement.

2. Different databases generated slightly different warranty costs, which in turn affected percentages by as much as 0.5–0.75 percent; in other words, warranty costs could be estimated to no more than ±0.5–0.75 percent. This significant finding indicated that the databases were not reliable.

3. Several definitions of warranty costs were used.

4. Errors in database entries amounted to approximately $250,000 per year (slightly less than 1 percent).

5. Field service personnel wrongly charged maintenance repair costs (not covered by warranty) or replacement of manuals (not covered by warranty) to warranty. This was a goodwill gesture to please the customer.

6. There was a great geographical variation in warranty costs for the same unit. Further analysis revealed that only three or four hospitals accounted for as much as 30–40 percent of the monthly warranty cost. The famous Pareto effect was at work.

7. Some field service engineers routinely replaced several parts when only one part had failed.

8. Warranty costs for the West Coast showed a regular increase in the last two months of the year (a period when hospitals

routinely called field service personnel for maintenance even if the equipment was in good working order).

9. For one particular unit, as much as 30–40 percent of the failures was attributable to two parts that regularly experienced problems during assembly. Further investigation revealed that these two parts (produced by two vendors) had caused problems during assembly for the past three years. Corrective actions written in early 2005 were still open more than 14 months later.

10. In 2005, several field change notices were introduced. These notices are issued when a failure is noticed in either the design or a part (often software). Such notices are very costly to implement because when they are issued they apply to the install base that in some cases might involve upward of 300 or more units. If a large percentage of these units are still under warranty, the cost can easily climb to hundreds of thousands of dollars.

11. Some parts delivered to the field service engineer arrived damaged (because of poor packaging) and had to be returned, thus adding additional shipping costs and wasted time for the field engineer who occasionally had to return a part two or three times. Oddly enough, the yearly cost of this double and sometimes triple shipment was not computed but was estimated to be at least $250,000–$350,000 (the additional cost to the customer was not computed).

12. Customer training was incorrectly charged to warranty cost.

13. One of the most bizarre findings was that on a few occasions warranty cost was recorded in the database for equipment *that had not yet been delivered.* What is more incomprehensible is that when the error was noted, it was impossible to correct it. More accurately, one could not convince the manager in charge of the database to correct the error without starting yet another problem-solving team.

14. A couple of problems that had been detected during the design phase but had not been corrected for the sake of satisfying the schedule were also responsible for some of the warranty repairs.

15. Approximately 15–18 percent of all parts under warranty that were returned from the field were found to have no

problems when tested at the return center. Further investigation revealed two interesting findings: (1) the tests performed at the return center were all too often inadequate and verified only the most basic functionality, such as whether the light came on, and (2) field engineers returned and replaced good parts for no apparent reason, thus adding to the warranty cost.

16. In a move to reduce cost and supposedly improve efficiency, field service zones were reduced in August 2005 from five to four (thus increasing the ratio of equipment per field service engineer). As a result of this reorganization, several experienced field engineers resigned. Although most field engineers still had many years of experience, this was not true for a couple of products with above-average warranty costs. For one particularly complex product there was only one or two experienced field engineers. Inexperienced field engineers working on this complex equipment tended to order more parts than were needed and/or misdiagnosed the problem, resulting in delays. The team was unable to determine the additional warranty costs to the company of this last item.

As can be seen in this list, at least 16 factors were found to be directly or indirectly linked to warranty cost and/or increased warranty cost. Some could be easily resolved, others would take several months, and most would never be resolved, because the managers responsible for the implementation of the corrective action did not consider it a primary responsibility.

When during a quarterly meeting this list of "causes" was reported, management did not seem very interested in the information and instead focused on the question, "Will you be able to achieve your target of $3.7 million in savings by the end of 2007?" When it was reported in mid-2006 that only $1.2 million in warranty savings could reasonably be expected to be achieved, management concluded that the team had failed and should have asked for more help to achieve its goal. Attempts to explain that the $3.7 million in savings had been unrealistic and based on erroneous assumptions and data were ignored. The figure had been engraved in the company's hoshin plan, and nothing could be done to reverse the situation. It was more convenient and expeditious to blame someone for savings of only $1.2 million out of an arbitrary figure of $3.7 million. When sales figures did not look good for the 2007–2008 season, 20 people were laid off. The savings had to be achieved one way or another, and the company

> had been losing $30 million–$35 million for the past five years. The executive managers are still with the company, although a director was eventually let go, presumably for failure to achieve (unrealistic) objectives.

SOME LESSONS LEARNED

Almost 55 years ago, Peter Drucker wrote an influential book entitled *The Practice of Management* (1954). Drucker, who acknowledged the influence of earlier writers such as Henri Fayol (1914), Mary Parker Follett (1920s and 1930s), Chester I. Barnard (1930s), and Elton Mayo (1930s and 1940s), covers a broad range of managerial issues. Chapter 28, "Making Decisions," should be required reading for all managers. Many of the suggestions on decision making presented by Drucker in 1954 are directly related to our warranty cost reduction case study. Drucker's recommendations are as follows:

1. Choosing the right question is much more important than finding the right answer.

2. Strategic decisions (unlike Mintzberg, Drucker believed in their importance) should never be made through problem solving, because problem-solving tools can only be used to find the right answer to a problem, whereas strategic decisions involve asking the right question(s).

3. Drucker also explains that decision making consists of five phases: (a) defining the real problem, (b) analyzing and classifying the problem to know who will need to be consulted prior to reaching a decision (that is, defining the key players), (c) developing alternate solutions, (d) deciding on the best solution, and (e) converting the decision into effective action.

4. Drucker also suggests that "selling a solution" is a waste of time and only indicates that the wrong people were consulted during the third phase (developing alternate solutions).

5. Drucker provides many other suggestions that are often better than what Six Sigma professionals suggest today.

Applying Drucker's methodology, we see that, as was suggested by the Master Black Belt in the early phases, the warranty cost reduction project was faced with several difficulties early on; it was a wicked problem.

Unless you already have a very good idea of the nature of the problem and know what Drucker calls the "critical factors"—the factors that will have to be changed *before* anything else is achieved or effectively acted upon—you will not be able to identify the key players and/or critical factors necessary to ensure that proposed solutions will be acted upon effectively and in a timely manner. Experience shows that during the early phases of problem definition, one often does not know what key manager(s) and or critical factors will be needed to effectively implement the yet to be proposed solutions to a problem. These steps can only evolve as one starts analyzing data, interviewing people, and charting processes. The 16 issues associated with warranty costs, many of which could be considered critical factors, were only uncovered after months of investigation; some (for example, problems with databases) were discovered accidentally during the course of the investigation.

A better approach would be to first carefully analyze the problem by collecting relevant information (data), mapping processes (if needed), analyzing the data, and interviewing process owners. In other words, identify the critical factors and then determine which manager(s) will be needed to resolve the problem(s). These key individuals will be needed to define an acceptable solution that will require no "selling" when the time comes to propose answers.

One should also be cautious of very large or broad-scope projects. The warranty cost reduction project seemed to have a well-defined scope (reduce warranty costs within one year), but actually the scope was very broad because it covered six products of various complexities, a point that has only been alluded to in this discussion. The perceived problem as stated by management was wrongly stated. The fact that warranty costs had been rising over a period of 12 months was easily explained by the fact that seven new products had been introduced. What the analysis revealed was that there were many other problems associated with warranty accounting, warranty maintenance as practiced by field service engineers, shipment of parts, and database errors. If anything, the warranty costs could have occupied at least three teams analyzing two products each; however, it is possible that these three teams would not have achieved as much as the one team did. Moreover, it is unlikely that the three teams could have achieved the required synergy to uncover the 16 factors listed earlier. The project occupied two people for approximately 13–14 months of nearly continuous analysis. And although the project resulted in many findings, management was expecting one or perhaps two key answers that would magically resolve the warranty cost "problem." Such was not the case, because, in part, the team did not have the authority to require managers to look into problems identified in their areas, and management was not willing to implement proposed solutions, because they perceived the problem as someone else's problem. They had other tactical priorities.

It is amusing to note that as the team leader had predicted, warranty costs did come down. In fact, for a brief period in late 2006 and early 2007, warranty costs did come down on their own without anybody doing anything (this mystery was never resolved except to suggest that cycles do tend to characterize the "behavior" of many processes). But as of late 2007 and 2008, overall warranty costs were back up to above 11 percent; the cycle was repeating and nothing had been achieved except that someone else (working alone this time) had been assigned the same problem and was in the process of rediscovering some of the same issues. Ironically, the warranty costs for a new product released in 2008 were running at slightly over 12 percent. The reader should not be surprised to learn that with regard to warranty cost reduction at this company, it is *more of the same.*

Annotated Bibliography

Altshuller, Genrich S. *Creativity as an Exact Science: The Theory of the Solution of Inventive Problems.* New York: Gordon and Breach Science Publishers, 1984.

Although this is an interesting book, it is not easy to read and is a bit specialized. It is probably more useful for a design engineer or a research scientist who wants to know how to innovate or invent. This is the book that influenced the TRIZ movement. Altshuller quotes Alex Osborn ("Brainstorming," 11–13), but he points out that brainstorming "is effective only for the solution of simple tasks" (13). It is well suited for organizational problems but not for inventive problems.

Brightman, Harvey L. *Problem Solving: A Logical and Creative Approach.* Atlanta: Business Publishing Division, College of Business Administration, Georgia State University, 1980.

This difficult-to-find and generally unknown book is one of the best on the subject of problem solving. It is impossible to summarize a book full of excellent suggestions; nonetheless, the following quotations should give the reader an idea of Brightman's valuable contribution.

Under a paragraph labeled "Schedulitis" (the disease of too many meetings and too many schedules), Brightman says this about managers: "A manager can become so engrossed in daily routine that he or she fails to see that *the primary job is problem solving.* As protection against the confusion, doubt, and ambiguity associated with real problems, this type of manager opts to avoid these unpleasantries by pointing to a full calendar. If the calendar is examined closely, one may find that the manager's time is taken up with many *non-managerial duties* . . . successful managers must also recognize that problem solving is an important professional skill" (5, emphasis added).

"By way of definition, the technical name for facts is data and the technical name for potential solutions is hypotheses" (9).

Chapter 2, "Constraints to Problem Solving," is a must-read for anyone but especially for Six Sigma Black Belts who might think they know everything about problem solving. Brightman identifies several cultural constraints, as well as organizational, managerial, and individual constraints, to problem solving. No wonder many problems remain unsolved!

"Don't accept facts or assumptions without challenging them. Never accept someone else's definition of a problem. Make the problem your own. Be a 'whys-guy'" (92).

"Remember, words are not the events themselves; rather, they are a translation of the events into language. No translation is perfect. In diagnosing a problem, be skeptical of words—inquire into their meaning. Beware the translator!" (100).

Brightman points out that some of the more important organizational barriers to innovation are the following:

1. Highly stable organizational environments
2. Overreliance on SOPs (standard operating procedures)
3. Highly centralized organization
4. Preoccupation with status and its associated symbols

Dorner, Dietrich. *The Logic of Failure*. Cambridge, MA: Perseus Books, 1996.

This excellent book covers several major topics including problem solving, training (verbal intelligence), and planning. Some of Dorner's valuable comments on problem solving and training are summarized here.

Dorner suggests that, sometimes, more thinking and less action is the better choice (17). He uses computer models to show how people try to solve problems. Dorner notes that when dealing with models, people act the same as in real life: They tend to act without prior analysis of a situation, they fail to anticipate side effects and long-term repercussions (consequences of systems), they assume that the absence of immediate negative effects means they have taken the correct steps, they tend to get over-involved in "projects" and fail to see emerging changes, and they are prone to cynical reactions (18).

Good participants (in model-solving problems) often reflect on their own behavior, comment critically on their decisions, and are not afraid to modify their decisions (26). Dorner also found that under time pressure, people tend to apply an overdose of established measures (emphasis on linear rather than nonlinear thinking) (33). People tend to act in terms of preestablished patterns (45).

A preoccupation with explicit goals "accounts for a great deal of bad planning and counterproductive measures" (52). On "repair service" behavior: A mayor may want to improve the "well-being of citizens" without having a clear idea of what that means. So the mayor (and problem solvers in general) goes out and looks for things that are malfunctioning and fixes them immediately. "A mayor who is guided by a randomly generated list of complaints risks giving far too much attention to relatively unimportant problems and either overlooking the truly important ones or failing to assess them properly" (59). Also, people tend to solve problems they know how to solve and not the ones that need to be solved (60). "Seizing on obvious or readily solved problems leads not to planned action but to helter-skelter responses first to one grievance, then to another" (63).

Dorner emphasizes the need to look at problems as systems. People tend to think of problem solving in terms of sequence: Solve one thing, then the next, and so forth. They do not account for side effects and repercussions of certain measures. People see systems "as a bundle of independent mini-systems" (87). One reason people deal with partial problems in isolation "is their preoccupation with the immediate goals" (87). He suggests that we avoid "reductive hypothesis," where everything is tied to one variable.

"Activity may foster an illusion of competence. By intervening massively, a person demonstrates his competence, his ability to take the situation in hand—he demonstrates it to himself at least" (181).

Dorner proposes some very interesting comments on the value of training. Three groups—two experimental and one control—were analyzed. The first two groups received instruction in some fairly complicated procedures for dealing with complex systems. One of the experimental groups was introduced to concepts like "system," "positive feedback," and "critical variables." The third or control group received some training on nebulous, ill-defined creative thinking. The first two groups agreed that the training had been "moderately" helpful. The control group felt that it was a waste of time. Why did the first two groups who had been trained with useless techniques find the training somewhat helpful? "The training gave them what I would call 'verbal intelligence' in the field of solving complex problems. Equipped with lots of shiny new concepts, they were able to talk about their thinking, their actions, and the problems they were facing. This gain in eloquence left no mark at all on their performance, however. . . . The ability to talk about something does not necessarily reflect in the ability to deal with it in reality" (196).

Lindbloom, Charles. "The Science of Muddling Through." *Public Administration Review* 19, no. 2 (1959): 79–88.

This influential article questions the use of the so-called rational method in complex decision making. Lindbloom, who wrote his article at a time when the methodologies proposed by operations research and systems analysis were just emerging, suggests that these "rational-comprehensive" methodologies are not useful when dealing with complex administrative policy issues. Administrators and policy makers, he suggests, must often "muddle through" a complex problem using what he refers to as "successive limited comparisons." Lindbloom's comments also apply to complex (interdepartmental) problems found in most industries.

7

Humanizing the Work Environment: A Recipe for Success

In economic history, equilibrium is the exception rather than the rule. A free market restores equilibrium only to break it down again, and to set in motion a new sequence of imbalances and instabilities with all the troubles that follow in their train. . . . In economic history, planners and managers are taught to prevent the last crisis from happening again. The next one is always different.

—David Hackett Fischer
The Great Wave: Price Revolutions and the Rhythm of History

Over the past 30 years, multinational corporations and the millions of individuals throughout the world employed by these Leviathans have had to continually face periodic business challenges caused by the perennial cycles of a capitalistic world economy. Globalization, a phenomenon known by certain economists for at least 150 years but popularized by the press and government only since the early 1980s, was an attempt to react to what Joseph Schumpeter referred to as the inherent destructive cycles of capitalism.[50] By expanding new markets and shifting their production abroad, multinationals found ways to

---

50. The theory of business cycles has been studied since at least the 1920s. Schumpeter's work is one of the most famous books on the subject (see the reference in the annotated bibliography).

constantly feed the vast machinery of the industrial world while at the same time improve their profit margins, at least until 2008.

One of the unfortunate consequences of globalization is that workers in the United States and Europe and also Latin America must now compete with workers in China, Vietnam, Thailand, the Dominican Republic, and other developing nations—countries with very different socioeconomic and healthcare systems. As more and more companies took advantage of globalization, worldwide competition became more fierce. In an effort to continuously improve efficiency, reduce cycle time, improve productivity, and reduce cost, companies began to adopt popular methods of lean manufacturing in the early 1980s. Jobs that were once performed by two or three individuals were now performed by one person. As we have seen in previous chapters, savings generated by lean manufacturing are often in sharp contrast with (or are a direct consequence of) the anti-lean managerial behavior required of today's manager and the ensuing extension of the workweek. Managers are now asked to use a variety of software tools to generate a multitude of reports, maintain certification to multiple international and national standards, perform internal audits to ensure that workers follow detailed standard operating procedures, and generate report upon report of seemingly endless metrics. As Richard Farson noted some years ago, "The confused manager, careening from trend to trend, cannot become an effective leader as long as he or she continues to believe in simplistic techniques. But a manager who can appreciate the absurdities and paradoxes of business relationships and organizations is surely going to be less vulnerable to fashion and therefore stronger as a leader."[51]

The need to solve problems weekly, if not daily, prompted Farson to write that since many of today's problems are not really problems but rather predicaments (see the discussions on wicked problems and the art of muddling through in Chapter 6), analytical skills would not be helpful in solving them, because predica-

---

51. Richard Farson, *Management of the Absurd: Paradoxes in Leadership* (New York: Simon & Schuster, 1996), p. 13.

ments require interpretive thinking, which requires the ability to put a larger frame around a situation (that is, different contexts).

As corporations strove to squeeze more output from their workers, the quality of work life steadily began to decline. Indeed, the development of the work environment over the past 40 years has not alleviated an already stressful situation.[52] The development of the cubicle in 1968 by Robert Propst, originally intended to be an agreeable work environment that would allow creativity and innovation to flourish, was transformed, much to the chagrin of its inventor, into the generally despised work cell derogatorily known as "cube farms."[53] The opportunity to have potentially more innovative and creative employees was easily trumped by the shortsighted vision of decision makers blinded by the economic and real estate efficiency of cubicles. And yet, researchers have long stated that in order to be more creative, productive, and enjoy a better quality of life, people need periods of what the Italian sociologist Domenico De Masi has called "creative idleness."[54] This ability to reach a state of creative and productive "flow" as described by Mihaly Csikszentmihalyi was

52. See the work by the American Institute of Stress, http://www.stress. org/job.htm?AIS=8b17cfcf7f050f32badfaf7ad349a5d2. See also the many contributions by Dr. Paul J. Rosch, editor of *Stress Medicine*, published by John Wiley and Sons in England, and the monthly newsletter *Health and Stress*, published by the American Institute for Stress.

53. The commercialization of the office cubicle is said to have first occurred in 1968. Robert Propst, who worked as a designer for Herman Miller, wanted to find ways to improve productivity. Thus, he designed the Action Office, a dynamic modular-type office that allowed for privacy and contained plenty of adjustable shelves to allow workers to stand up as well as spread out their paperwork. The Action Office was not designed to pack as many people as possible in as small an area as possible (known as cube farms); that evolution, at least in the United States, was driven by economics and new (in the 1960s) tax laws. Propst himself later refer to the metamorphosis of his Action Office as a "monolithic insanity."

54. Domenico De Masi, *O Ozio Criativo* (Creative Idleness) (Rio de Janeiro: Sextante, 2000).

unfortunately postponed indefinitely. Let us hope enlightened business leaders will soon recognize, as the renowned philosopher Bertrand Russell did over 75 years ago, the importance of creative idleness.[55]

Similar observations could be made regarding cell phones, laptops, and the Internet. These inventions have many positive effects allowing people to work from the comfort of their home. However, it is also true that like any other technology, they all have negative side effects. Managers can now reach their employees on their cell phones after work hours, and, in the case of companies with national or international offices, inconsiderate managers living in one time zone can schedule meetings that would require a 6 a.m. attendance for someone living in another time zone. All of these technological features designed to supposedly "improve" one's lifestyle have in fact lengthened the workweek to an average of 45–50 hours for many professionals.[56]

---

55. Mihaly Csikszentmihalyi, *Flow—The Psychology of Optimal Experience* (New York: Harper, 1990). Useful links include http://en.wikipedia. org/wiki/Flow_(psychology), http://www.brainchannels.com/ thinker/mihaly.html, http://edutechwiki.unige.ch/en/Flow_theory, and http://www.ebl.org/flow_article.html.

In 1932 Bertrand Russell published an interesting essay entitled "In Praise of Idleness." In it, Russell proposes, among other things, "that a great deal of harm is being done in the modern world by belief in the virtuousness of work, and that the road to happiness and prosperity lies in an organized diminution of work." The article can be found at http://www.zpub.com/notes/idle.html.

56. See also "Work-Life Balance" at http://en.wikipedia.org/wiki/ Work-life_balance, Madeleine Bunting's book Willing Slaves: How the Overwork Culture Is Ruling Our Lives (London: HarperCollins, 2004), and the article by Audrey Gillian, "Work until You Drop: How the Long Hours Culture Is Killing Us," Manchester Guardian, August 20, 2005, http://www.guardian.co.uk/uk/2005/aug/20/ britishidentity.health.

See also Juliet B. Schor's groundbreaking study, *The Overworked American: The Unexpected Decline of Leisure* (New York: Basic Books [HarperCollins], 1992).

Aware that employees are faced with many stressful situations, companies have been very creative at finding ways to motivate their workers to more readily accept the challenge of a stressful work environment. Companies have traditionally relied on the help of consultants for assistance in motivational issues. However, faced with difficult economic times, companies are now using the vast, readily available resource of internal human capital to develop new organizational paradigms.

WE KEEP TRYING TO MOTIVATE PEOPLE . . .

Motivational studies started in the late 1930s, were popular in the 1940s, and continue to this day.[57] Not so long ago, in a more prosperous time when companies could afford elaborate and pricey employee surveys, it was not unusual for companies to hire a consulting firm to assess the "mood" of its employees. Oftentimes, one of the consequences of these company-wide surveys was that executive managers would segregate themselves for two to three days in a retreat environment to review the survey results with consultants and develop a new way of doing business. The hiring of a motivational speaker often complements the two-day event. The purpose of the "motivational lecture" is to bring the audience, or at least the majority of its participants, to a state of near-ecstatic enthusiasm. Presumably, this heightened state of euphoria is perceived as a necessary motivational prerequisite to implement the changes that will, in theory, turn around the company. Unfortunately, after the employee returns to work to face the daily realities of too many meetings, conflict resolution, and weekly or monthly problem solving, the initial state of euphoria, if such a state was ever achieved, dissipates and a "normal" status-quo behavior rapidly reasserts itself. Why?

Motivational programs rarely deliver what they promise for the following reasons: (1) these programs are punctual and

---

57. Warren G. Bennis and Edgar H. Schein, eds., *Leadership and Motivation: Essays of Douglas McGregor* (Cambridge, MA: Massachusetts Institute of Technology Press, 1966).

short-lived, the effect lasting only a few hours or days, and (2) the generic nature of these motivational programs that assume all participants will react the same way (much as a drug is supposed to relieve a symptom with equal effect on all patients) is based on a false assumption. As was shown long ago, people are moved by different motivational forces.

Motivational programs and other related programs, such as leadership development, should focus on developing positive energy and favorable conditions for professional satisfaction rather than on activities that supposedly bring a false sense of motivation to their participants. Some years ago, Russell Ackhoff reached similar conclusions when he observed that "improvement programs should be directed at getting what people want, not, as is usually the case, *at getting rid of what they do not want.*"[58] Indeed, one of the major challenges facing corporations is that they will need to learn to listen attentively to their workers—the very people working with the product and the processes producing these products. As Ackhoff observes,

> The higher the quality of work life the producers of products or services enjoy, the higher the quality of products or services they produce. These two types of quality are closely related. Those who do not enjoy a high quality of work life transform their dissatisfaction with their work into the poor quality of products or services they produce.

Once planners and managers give up the idea of redesigning the work of others and, instead, give them an opportunity to design their own work and work environment, employees have no difficulty bringing about changes that lead to significant improvements in their quality of work life. Workers are more likely than planners or managers to know what dissatisfies them, what causes their dissatisfactions, and what to do about them.

---

58. Russell A. Ackhoff, *The Democratic Corporation* (New York: Oxford University Press, 1994), p. 98 (emphasis added).

Participation, which is a form of self-determination, is itself a major source of satisfaction and therefore of improved quality of life.[59]

It has been 15 years since Ackhoff wrote his book, and companies still tend to promote leaders who can solve problems instead of focusing on developing leaders who can appreciate and know how to tap the human capital surrounding them.[60]

APPRECIATIVE INQUIRY: AN ANTIDOTE TO PROBLEM SOLVING

Finding solutions to all sorts of problems seems to be the mantra of many managers in today's organizations. Managers are often evaluated on their ability to rapidly and efficiently resolve conflict and solve all sorts of daily problems. But is it really wise for a company to rely so heavily on problem-solving specialists, and could such a behavior induce negative side effects? Starting in the 1970s, some organizational development researchers—notably early contributors David Cooperrider, coordinator of the Business as a Worldwide Benefit Agent program at Ohio's Case Western University, and Suresh Srivastva—began to suggest that companies should consider a totally different approach. Cooperrider and others observed that companies that had a strategic vision and were focused on solving daily management and operational problems tended to remain stagnant. On the other hand, companies that focused on their successes and strengths could more quickly and innovatively adapt to change. Thus was born the influential organizational methodology (some would say philosophy) known as Appreciative Inquiry (AI).

---

59. Ackhoff, *The Democratic Corporation*, pp. 74, 77, 78.

60. We do not mean to suggest that Russell Ackhoff was the first author to raise the issue of a democratic corporation; countless others had reached similar conclusions long before Ackhoff. The field of appreciative inquiry, for example, although not necessarily directly connected to Ackhoff's theme, offers a similar participatory approach.

We are not suggesting that AI will be a panacea to all industries, nor do we believe that any organization would be ready to adopt its principles. Nevertheless, we do believe that some of the suggestions proposed by AI are worth outlining. The following is but a cursory look at the fundamental principles proposed by AI. For a more detailed account, the reader is referred to the many books available on the subject.

AI should not be confused with the cheerleading aspects of some motivational practices. As Kathleen and Paul Connolly demonstrated years ago, few employees respond well to cheerleading:

> Contrary to what some may believe, good morale does not always lead to positive motivation. Positive motivation does not always lead to high productivity. . . . Satisfied employees are not always effective and effective employees are not always satisfied. Morale is thus not a sure road to improved productivity. While positive morale makes management easier, it is not directly linked to effective performance.[61]

The term "appreciation" is meant to convey *recognition* as well as *enhancement* or *amelioration*, whereas "inquiry" refers to the need to explore and *discover* new possibilities for change. AI is therefore meant to build on past and present positive practices that are to be found within an organization, its various departments, and most importantly, its people. Rather than rely on consultants to advise an organization as to what is needed to improve, AI looks inwardly and depends on the knowledge base and human capital of the employees to create or transform it into a better organization.

---

61. Kathleen Groll Connolly and Paul M. Connolly, *Competing for Employees* (Lexington, MA: Lexington Books, 1991), pp. 35, 36. See also the suggestion of Arie de Geus that a company should be a "living company." Arie de Geus, *The Living Company*. Foreword by Peter M. Senge (Boston: Harvard Business School Press, 1997).

This focus on positive actions that is derived from the internal wisdom of employees is in sharp contrast to a corporate culture that focuses on the hiring of consultants (or deploys a flock of corporate directors or young executives) to solve real or imaginary *problems* or resolve real or imaginary *conflicts*, two sources of negative energy. The AI approach consists of recording, through interviews and discussions with as many employees as possible, past and present events of positive corporate achievements. This includes recording not only successes of individual employees but also successful customer relation stories, supplier relations, and all other positive experiences. In contrast to other methods of planning, AI does not consider weak or negative points but rather emphasizes everything that can be considered as a competitive advantage.

Several companies such as British Airways, Avon, Hunter Douglas, NASA, and McDonald's have used AI to promote organizational changes. AI consists of four ongoing phases reminiscent of other methodologies: discovery, dream, design, and destiny. The discovery phase consists of extensive interviews designed to identify what has worked well in the past or what an organization is particularly good at. These success stories are meant to serve as a source of inspiration for planning for the future. An example of what could potentially be explored as a good discovery was identified in Chapter 5 in "Case Study I: Estimated Time to Repair." The reader will recall that, after interviewing a couple of quality engineers, it was learned that in prior years more field engineers had been used to serve clients. Unfortunately, a reorganization designed to allegedly bring more efficiency and generate savings had been implemented; this act was attributed in part to an increase in response time and a related increase in customer dissatisfaction. It is not unusual to learn from employees that a process was "better" (that is, fewer errors or customer complaints) before the implementation of some cost-saving process.

In the dream phase, people are encouraged to envision how processes could be improved, what new style of leadership would be required, and what resources would be needed to achieve these future objectives.

The design phase, as its name implies, consists of selecting processes (for example, management practices, human resource process, customer support, process measurement metrics, and production processes) and planning their implementation. The destiny phase is where the proposed design is initiated and where strategies are created to transform the dream in practical terms. What distinguishes AI from other models of business reorganization is that AI incorporates as part of its reinventing process the aspirations and desires of employees; in other words, AI is built from the base rather than being imposed from above. AI is considered as one of the most innovative and promising tools for organizational management today.

CONCLUSION

As we wrote this book, the economies of many nations were experiencing a severe recession. At a time when most economists here and abroad are predicting increases in unemployment rates for 2009 and perhaps beyond, talks on humanizing the work environment may seem anachronistic. Yet, it is precisely during such crises that important visionary and even revolutionary decisions must be made. Companies must not only act boldly but also act wisely and with sensitivity. Does it make sense, for example, for a company to invest in a period of severe economic crisis and as part of its Visual Factory program, as much as $150,000 on an information system that includes at least half a dozen large television screens to display messages and various performance metrics 24 hours a day? One cannot deny that all those television monitors may look good for visiting customers (which was the primary intent), and they may even give an appearance of total control. But even if the information displayed is accurate (which is questionable), would it not be better for the company to spend the money on improving the quality of work life of its workers? The company in question employs a high percentage of temporary employees who are paid minimum wage. One of the corporate policies requires that all employees (temporary and full time) wear protective shoes that cost, on average, around $60. Although vouchers are offered to full-time employees, the company does not reimburse its temporary workers, because "it would cost too much money." When someone mentioned that asking an employee who earns $9 an hour to pay $50–$60 for a pair of shoes would be particularly onerous, the reply was that the employee could buy shoes for $20–$25. However, cheap shoes would likely be uncomfortable, especially when one is required to stand for eight or more hours. Obviously, this was not the concern of management. This difficult-to-understand rationality proposes that spending upward of $150,000 (the equivalent of about 2500–3000 pairs of shoes) on television screens and software to display what could be conceived as propaganda messages is a better investment than investing a fraction of that cost to ensure that employees are comfortable while performing their work. So much for worker appreciation.

More themes could have been presented. For example, companies that obsessively attempt to reach optimal efficiency may not realize that they could be flirting with danger. A potential problem encountered by these so-called lean companies is that the slightest variation or unpredictability in schedule, operations, or customer orders can quickly affect the tightly maintained equilibrium. Unable to respond because of insufficient (others might say optimum) resources—resources that may have been recently eliminated because of some cost-saving kaizen event— the company finds that the unexpected disturbance to the system soon amplifies and can become a major crisis overnight. In an attempt to economize a few dollars or euros, companies are often confronted with the painful task of spending large amounts of money to react, rectify, or adjust to an unforeseen event that could have been avoided if only the penny-pinching philosophy had not been adopted. When faced with such crises, many companies tend to overreact by throwing people at the problem, thereby wiping out in a few weeks the savings generated by any recently implemented kaizen (cost-saving) event.[62]

---

62. A *kaizen event* is a form of continuous process improvement. In the United States, kaizen events tend to focus on rapid improvements and rarely exceed 5–10 days' duration. One should note that new problems occasionally emerge soon after a kaizen event has been implemented.

We could have also talked about companies that are top-heavy with restless managers who have nothing better to do than to issue directives to already overworked employees. The business literature tends to focus on the messianic leader who supposedly has led a company to success, or as of 2008–2009 to failure. More often than not, it is the people reporting to the messianic leader who are the source of the problem. Over the years we have observed many instances where the ill-advised decisions of one or two high-ranking corporate individuals have had a disastrous impact on the financial performance of a company, not to mention the nefarious rippling effects such decisions have had on morale. We may one day revisit these themes.

Annotated Bibliography

Bennis, Warren G., and Edgar H. Schein (eds.). *Leadership and Motivation: Essays of Douglas McGregor*. Cambridge, MA: Massachusetts Institute of Technology Press, 1966.

McGregor cites a 1939 study on behavior by Lewin and Lippitt (in the chapter "Patterns of Aggressive Behavior"). Many of the cited works on human motivation are from the early 1940s. Referring to the Scanlon Plan, McGregor observes that "rewards become less effective the more remote in time they are from the behavior that is rewarded" (136).

Cooperrider, David, Diana Whitney, and Jacqueline Stavross. *Appreciative Inquiry Handbook for Leaders of Change*. New York: Crown Custom, 2005.

This book is *the* reference for appreciative inquiry. Cooperrider reviews many success stories and explains how to effectively implement the methodology.

Csikszentmihalyi, Mihaly. *Flow—The Psychology of Optimal Experience*. New York: Harper, 1990.

For the past 25 years, Csikszentmihalyi studied what he refers to as "excellent experiences." According to him, a state of flow can be reached while performing any activity. Some of the characteristics of a state of flow are maximum concentration, the sensation that time passes without our realizing it, and the use of our intellect on some specific ability. To be "in flow" means to reinvigorate ourselves and thus increase our odds of being happier.

de Geus, Arie. *The Living Company.* Foreword by Peter M. Senge. Boston: Harvard Business School Press, 1997.

De Geus was a high-ranking executive at Shell for 38 years. For de Geus, a living company is one that has sensitivity, cohesion and identity, tolerance and conservative financing (9). He quotes an interesting study that was conducted in 1983 at Shell (on a small sample of about 40 companies) that demonstrated that companies live to be only about 50 years old. To be more successful (that is, to live longer), de Geus claims a company must become a living company, that is, a learning company. Learning companies make continuous changes to adapt. Managers must learn to see the signals. Continuous change in the world requires continuous fundamental changes in the internal structures of a company (27).

Farson, Richard. *Management of the Absurd: Paradoxes in Leadership.* New York: Simon & Schuster, 1996.

We highly recommend this book. Farson covers a broad range of topics; some of his insights follow.

Once you find a management technique that works, give it up (4). Leaders cannot be trained but they can be educated. Training = development of skills and techniques. Education = information and knowledge, which "in the right hands can lead to understanding, even to wisdom" (155).

"True leaders are defined by the groups they are serving, and they understand the job as being interdependent with the group" (145). "Humility comes naturally to the best leaders . . . indeed, leaders are themselves often led and managed by their employees, from the bottom up—colleagues whose ideas, assistance, arguments, and sometimes dogged resistance have real influence" (146–147).

Fischer, David Hackett. *The Great Wave: Price Revolutions and the Rhythm of History*. New York: Oxford University Press, 1996.

"In economic history, equilibrium is the exception rather than the rule. A free market restores equilibrium only to break it down again, and to set in motion a new sequence of imbalances and instabilities with all the troubles that follow in their train." And again, "in our complex and highly integrated modern economies, there are no truly free markets any more. The free market of the twentieth century is an economic fiction. . . . The real question is not whether we should interfere with the market, but what sort of interference we should make, and who will make it, and what its extent will be" (252).

In view of the recent events on Wall Street, it is only appropriate that we include this quotation: "In economic history, planners and managers are taught to prevent the last crisis from happening again. The next one is always different" (253).

Lamprecht, James. *Quality and Power in the Supply Chain: What Industry Does for the Sake of Quality*. Boston: Butterworth-Heinemann, 2000.

Several themes are explored in this book: (1) the historical evolution of the "age of standardization" and the influence of military standards, (2) the nefarious effects of fads on companies, (3) the consequences of standardization, and (4) the need to transition to an "age of flexibility," as well as other related themes on customer-supplier relationships.

Lancaster, Lynne C., and David Stillman. *When Generations Collide*. New York: Collins Business, 2002.

The main theme of the book is on generational conflicts within a corporate environment. The authors address and define four categories of people who live and interact in an organization: the traditionalists, the baby boomers, Generation X, and the "old timers."

Martin, Chuck. *Tough Management.* New York: McGraw-Hill, 2005.

This book is based on a series of research with executives from several countries. Martin covers issues that are important to an executive's success in today's business world. He notes that an employee's perception of fairness is an important factor in determining whether a talented individual stays at or leaves an organization.

Naisbitt, John. *Mind Set!* New York: Collins, 2006.

The author of the best seller *Megatrends* provides the reader with a series of new trends and forecasts. Naisbitt makes a series of interesting comparisons about economic cycles and the ebb and flow of some industrialized products. He concludes that the growth of China's economy is bound to "collide" with globalization.

Schumpeter, Joseph A. *The Theory of Economic Development: An Inquiry into Profits, Capital, Credit, Interest, and the Business Cycle.* New York: Redvers Opie, 1961.

This classic book, published posthumously, explains the principles of business cycles that are typical of the inherent destructive and constructive tendencies of capitalism. See also *Capitalism, Socialism, and Democracy* (New York: Harper & Row, 1942).

8

Conclusion

Never trust the wind that swells your sails, it is always obsolete.

—Samuel Beckett
Mercier and Camier

W e have come to the end of our commentary without offering many specific solutions. While this might seem ironic, it is not illogical, because, after all, if we had all the answers, that would mean that we had uncovered the secret of how to reverse or modify human nature or prevent cycles from recurring. What we do hope is that managers will at least consider what we have observed before using a software application to manipulate (analyze?) the next set of metrics to be reviewed at their next meeting. Better yet, we hope that they at least attempt to resist the next managerial fad or to question their habits—in other words, modify their behavior.

A few weeks before the book was finished, one of the authors was vacationing in Seattle. One sunny day (a rare occurrence in Seattle), while the author was sitting at a restaurant with a view of Lake Washington, a group of four young men (whose ages ranged from late twenties to mid-thirties) sat at a table next to his. The young men appeared to be a mix of teachers, administrators, and/or students at a local university. One man dominated the conversation and spoke with a loud voice that made it impossible not to hear what he was saying. He was telling the others about various administrative and curriculum reorganizations the university was about to undertake. He then started to talk about his doctoral dissertation, and with great confidence he said something rather interesting. It sounded something like this, "More and more companies today want managers that can make instant decisions with little information."[63]

The author could not believe his ears; "instant decisions" was apparently the latest fad.[64] If that is true or even partly true, it could begin to explain the September 2008 Wall Street debacle that continues to reverberate throughout the world. Could it be possible that gigantic financial institutions were being led by highly paid executives who were particularly skillful in the art of making instantaneous decisions based on little information? This absurd explanation may not be that far-fetched. Given the present cost (estimated at one to two trillion dollars) to society (that is, American taxpayers and millions of others around the world), let us hope that this "new" fad of instantaneous decision making does not take off and help re-create more of the same financial disasters. The world economies could not survive another collapse. We hope that our book has helped the reader realize why things are often always the same. We also hope that the themes presented in the previous seven chapters help illustrate how these persistent habits could be avoided or reversed.

We recognize that new technologies will continue to be invented and used by industries to improve competitiveness,

---

63. The German psychologist Dietrich Dorner observed that "the less information gathered, the greater the readiness to act. And vice versa." *The Logic of Failure* (Cambridge, MA: Perseus Books, 1996), p. 101. Once again, nothing new under the sun.

64. A quick search on the Web revealed one short book by Zelma Barinov with the interesting title *How to Make Instant Decisions and Remain Happy & Sane: Using Your Inner Compass* (Bala Cynwyd, PA: Access Press, Self-Help, 1998). The authors have reviewed the table of contents but have not read the book.

financial results, and, hopefully, the quality of work life (which, alas, is so often ignored). Assessing the advantages and disadvantages of any new technology is a difficult task, for, as we have repeatedly demonstrated, it is impossible to predict the future. All we know for sure is that until we find a way to mitigate or eliminate their impact, economic cycles, by their very nature, will come and go. What was popular yesterday or even today may not be popular tomorrow. Aware of these obvious facts, business leaders should adopt new technologies only after carefully assessing their advantages and disadvantages. We hope we have shown in this book that when new technologies or methodologies are adopted, habits and practices, behaviors, and/or processes are invariably affected—sometimes for the better and sometimes for the worse. Thus, whenever something new is adopted, one must monitor its impact on the work environment or at least ensure within reason that the "new way" of doing business will not create more insane and wasteful work for all of us.

As we witness the end of an era epitomized by the collapse of multinationals such as General Motors and even giant financial organizations, perhaps the time has come to acknowledge the wisdom of Leopold Kohr, who, writing in a different context, suggested more than 50 years ago that "whenever something is wrong something is too big."[65] The executive leader who first recognizes the wisdom of the "less is more" philosophy and simultaneously offers a *reasonable* steady rate of return for investors while maintaining a "people-centric" positive work environment for employees may well become, ironically, the next "innovative"

---

65. Leopold Kohr, *The Breakdown of Nations* (New York: E.P. Dutton, 1957), p. xviii. Kohr was prophetically referring to the need for nation-states to be broken down into smaller states—something that has in fact occurred over the past 25–30 years.

trendsetter.[66] Returning to a more sensible and *stable* status, which would be desirable for all, will happen only when people:

- Have fewer meetings and conference calls
- Send fewer e-mails
- Shorten their PowerPoint presentations (or better yet, do away with PowerPoint presentations)
- Reduce the number of metrics to an absolute minimum
- Develop sensible and meaningful metrics
- Resist the temptation of opening senseless corrective actions
- End the questionable practice of requiring every supplier (even the most exemplary ones) to be ISO 9001 certified
- Avoid getting caught up in endless planning extrapolations (hoshin or otherwise) that are based on wishful or even mystical assumptions

In other words, people should simplify their daily routines by relying less on the use of software tools to overanalyze everything. For we can all agree that as of the end of 2008, things have stopped being the same.[67]

Irrespective of the current economic situation, the time to act and differentiate ourselves from others is now. Cycles will come and go, and the decision to act on or ignore trends is up to each one of us. To follow fads just to be up to date can be dangerous.

---

66. The Zen-like expression "less is more" has been attributed to the furniture designer Ludwig Mies Van Der Rohe (1886–1969). "Less is more" is not to be confused with the popular "do more with less" expression, which promotes doing more work with fewer resources and is an expression that is often used prior to announcing layoffs. In the last few decades, "do more with less" has come to convey not only the opposite meaning of "less is more" but also the opposite meaning of its original nineteenth-century intent.

67. See Peter S. Goodman, "Is the Lean Economy Turning Mean?" *New York Times*, March 8, 2008, http://www.nytimes.com/2008/03/02/business/02jobs.html.

Many companies have come to regret their actions, but they are so committed or involved with the new fad that they are reluctant to admit their errors and continue to stumble forward. The ability to question our habits, resist the temptation to copy others, and, above all, see things differently from others will be the challenges of the twenty-first century for all businesses.

Index

Belong to the Quality Community!

Established in 1946, ASQ is a global community of quality experts in all fields and industries. ASQ is dedicated to the promotion and advancement of quality tools, principles, and practices in the workplace and in the community.

The Society also serves as an advocate for quality. Its members have informed and advised the U.S. Congress, government agencies, state legislatures, and other groups and individuals worldwide on quality-related topics.

Vision

By making quality a global priority, an organizational imperative, and a personal ethic, ASQ becomes the community of choice for everyone who seeks quality technology, concepts, or tools to improve themselves and their world.

ASQ is...

- More than 90,000 individuals and 700 companies in more than 100 countries
- The world's largest organization dedicated to promoting quality
- A community of professionals striving to bring quality to their work and their lives
- The administrator of the Malcolm Baldrige National Quality Award
- A supporter of quality in all sectors including manufacturing, service, healthcare, government, and education
- YOU

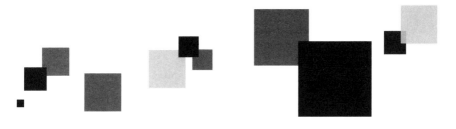

Visit www.asq.org for more information.

ASQ Membership

Research shows that people who join associations experience increased job satisfaction, earn more, and are generally happier*. ASQ membership can help you achieve this while providing the tools you need to be successful in your industry and to distinguish yourself from your competition. So why wouldn't you want to be a part of ASQ?

Networking

Have the opportunity to meet, communicate, and collaborate with your peers within the quality community through conferences and local ASQ section meetings, ASQ forums or divisions, ASQ Communities of Quality discussion boards, and more.

Professional Development

Access a wide variety of professional development tools such as books, training, and certifications at a discounted price. Also, ASQ certifications and the ASQ Career Center help enhance your quality knowledge and take your career to the next level.

Solutions

Find answers to all your quality problems, big and small, with ASQ's Knowledge Center, mentoring program, various e-newsletters, *Quality Progress* magazine, and industry-specific products.

Access to Information

Learn classic and current quality principles and theories in ASQ's Quality Information Center (QIC), *ASQ Weekly* e-newsletter, and product offerings.

Advocacy Programs

ASQ helps create a better community, government, and world through initiatives that include social responsibility, Washington advocacy, and Community Good Works.

Visit www.asq.org/membership for more information on ASQ membership.

*2008, The William E. Smith Institute for Association Research

ASQ Certification

ASQ certification is formal recognition by ASQ that an individual has demonstrated a proficiency within, and comprehension of, a specified body of knowledge at a point in time. Nearly 150,000 certifications have been issued. ASQ has members in more than 100 countries, in all industries, and in all cultures. ASQ certification is internationally accepted and recognized.

Benefits to the Individual

- New skills gained and proficiency upgraded
- Investment in your career
- Mark of technical excellence
- Assurance that you are current with emerging technologies
- Discriminator in the marketplace
- Certified professionals earn more than their uncertified counterparts
- Certification is endorsed by more than 125 companies

Benefits to the Organization

- Investment in the company's future
- Certified individuals can perfect and share new techniques in the workplace
- Certified staff are knowledgeable and able to assure product and service quality

Quality is a global concept. It spans borders, cultures, and languages. No matter what country your customers live in or what language they speak, they demand quality products and services. You and your organization also benefit from quality tools and practices. Acquire the knowledge to position yourself and your organization ahead of your competition.

Certifications Include
- Biomedical Auditor – CBA
- Calibration Technician – CCT
- HACCP Auditor – CHA
- Pharmaceutical GMP Professional – CPGP
- Quality Inspector – CQI
- Quality Auditor – CQA
- Quality Engineer – CQE
- Quality Improvement Associate – CQIA
- Quality Technician – CQT
- Quality Process Analyst – CQPA
- Reliability Engineer – CRE
- Six Sigma Black Belt – CSSBB
- Six Sigma Green Belt – CSSGB
- Software Quality Engineer – CSQE
- Manager of Quality/Organizational Excellence – CMQ/OE

Visit www.asq.org/certification to apply today!

ASQ Training

Classroom-based Training

ASQ offers training in a traditional classroom setting on a variety of topics. Our instructors are quality experts and lead courses that range from one day to four weeks, in several different cities. Classroom-based training is designed to improve quality and your organization's bottom line. Benefit from quality experts; from comprehensive, cutting-edge information; and from peers eager to share their experiences.

Web-based Training

Virtual Courses

ASQ's virtual courses provide the same expert instructors, course materials, interaction with other students, and ability to earn CEUs and RUs as our classroom-based training, without the hassle and expenses of travel. Learn in the comfort of your own home or workplace. All you need is a computer with Internet access and a telephone.

Self-paced Online Programs

These online programs allow you to work at your own pace while obtaining the quality knowledge you need. Access them whenever it is convenient for you, accommodating your schedule.

Some Training Topics Include
- Auditing
- Basic Quality
- Engineering
- Education
- Healthcare
- Government
- Food Safety
- ISO
- Leadership
- Lean
- Quality Management
- Reliability
- Six Sigma
- Social Responsibility

Visit www.asq.org/training for more information.